THE CHEETAH

BY NATHAN AASENG

Endangered Animals & Habitats

LUCENT BOOKS, INC.
SAN DIEGO, CALIFORNIA

Library of Congress Cataloging-in-Publication Data

Aaseng, Nathan.
    The cheetah / by Nathan Aaseng.
        p.   cm. — (Endangered animals & habitats)
    Includes bibliographical references (p.) and index.
    Summary: Describes this endangered animal including its
hunting for food on the African plain and the competition which it
faces, its reproduction and development, and the effect of humans
on its decline.
    ISBN 1-56006-680-6 (lib. bdg. : alk. paper)
    1. Cheetah—Juvenile literature. 2. Endangered species—Juvenile
literature. [1. Cheetah. 2. Endangered species.] I. Title. II. Series.
QL737.C23 A145 2000
599.75'9—dc21   99-050626

Contents

Introduction

A SPOTTED HEAD rises above the tall, sparse grass on the African plain. Standing on a termite mound, a cheetah stretches to her full height as she surveys the flat lands around her. The late afternoon sun beats down relentlessly, and most predators are at rest, waiting for the cool of the evening before beginning their hunt. But the cheetah is a hunter of the daytime. In a land filled with larger, stronger predators, she must take her opportunities when she can find them. Dependent on keen eyesight to locate prey, she hunts while the light is good.

The cheetah spots a group of small deerlike creatures known as Thomson's gazelles feeding a quarter mile away. Detecting no scent of a nearby predator, the gazelles eat calmly, with no apparent concern.

Eyes riveted on her prey, the cheetah silently, slowly creeps toward the gazelles. She stays low, and her spotted fur blends in well among the grasses. As she draws closer to the gazelles, her pace slows even further. Patience is the key to a successful hunt. The closer the cheetah can advance to her prey undetected, the greater the chance she will have a meal.

The cheetah creeps to within fifty yards (forty-six meters) and still the gazelles are unaware of her presence. In fact, several of them wander directly toward her as they nibble the grass. The cheetah stops and crouches even lower to the ground. As long as the gazelles are coming her way, she will not move again until the moment of attack.

One oblivious gazelle wanders a few yards away from the others. As the cheetah waits in ambush, she focuses on this animal. From this moment, the other gazelles do not exist for her. She will either kill this one or she will kill no gazelles on this hunt.

The gazelle approaches to within twenty yards. The cheetah does not move a muscle. Fifteen yards. The predator readies herself to spring. She could attack now, but at this point every step closer increases the odds that she will catch this elusive animal. Two more steps. One more.

Suddenly, the cheetah explodes from her hiding place, triggering one of the most breathtaking sights in the natural world. Startled out of its wits, the gazelle springs straight up in the air and then bolts in the opposite direction. A Thomson's gazelle is one of the fastest animals in the world and can sprint at speeds of forty miles (sixty-four kilometers) per hour. But the cheetah is faster. Her legs become a blur to the human eyes as she accelerates to a speed of three long strides per second and quickly closes in on her prey.

The cheetah, the fastest land animal in the world, can sprint at speeds up to seventy miles per hour.

The gazelle senses doom and darts from side to side. Even at this incredible speed, the cheetah follows every turn and twist of her prey. Desperately, the gazelle makes a breakneck stop and dashes in the opposite direction. But the cheetah wheels with equal grace. She quickly makes up the short distance she lost in the turn and swipes at the gazelle's hind legs with one paw. The gazelle trips and tumbles to the ground. Immediately, the cheetah pounces on it, grabbing its throat in its jaws.

The spectacular speed and majestic grace of a cheetah in full pursuit of a fast prey is one of the most thrilling sights in nature. Unfortunately, it is becoming an increasingly rare sight. If the experts are correct, future generations may never witness the beauty of a cheetah stretched to its full length in midstride. Unless action is taken soon, the only evidence that such a marvel ever existed will be a few canisters of fading film.

1

Decline of the Cheetah

THE FOSSIL RECORD suggests that the cheetah is one of the oldest of the large cats. Several species of cheetahs existed in the past, although scientists differ as to whether there have been three or four species. The earliest cheetahs were similar in form to those that exist today, only much larger. These lion-sized cheetahs roamed much of Europe and Asia, perhaps as long ago as 4 or 5 million years.

Some scientists, such as researchers at the American University in Washington, D.C., believe that the fossil evidence supports not only the idea that cheetahs once thrived in North America but also that they actually originated there. Other experts, such as Bernhard Grzimek of the Frankfurt Zoo, believe that there is no evidence that cheetahs ever lived in North America. They argue that fossil bones found in North America that closely resemble those of a cheetah are actually a form of cougar.

Fossil records indicate that cheetahs gradually evolved into smaller forms that spread through the Middle East and Africa. The only surviving species of cheetah is known as *Acinonyx jubatus*.

Spotted one

The cheetah's common name comes from *chitah*, a Hindi word that means "spotted one." Spots are one of the keys both to classifying cheetahs and to identifying them as individuals. All cheetahs have spots that are rounder, smaller, and more uniform than those of other spotted cats. They also have a characteristic stripe in the corner of their eyes that looks like a tear drop. Despite sharing the characteristic of spots with several other cat species, cheetahs are not closely related to any other species. So different are cheetahs from other cats that some zoologists believe that these creatures belong in a subfamily all their own.

The spotting pattern may appear to be the same on all cheetahs and, to the casual observer, one cheetah looks very much like any other. However, researchers who spend their days observing cheetahs, can readily tell individuals apart by differences in the spotting patterns, particularly on the face, neck, chest, and tail.

Small, round, even spots and stripes from the inner corner of the eye distinguish the cheetah from other spotted cats.

Some biologists have used these subtle differences in coat patterns to further divide cheetahs into as many as seven subspecies. (Subspecies are a group of animals, usually separated from other populations of the same species

Spots: Key to Identity

The "king" cheetah is an example of a false reliance on coat pattern variations to determine differences in species. In 1926 hunters in what is today known as Zimbabwe came across a cheetah sporting stripes on its back. When others were later discovered with the same marking, some biologists designated this a separate species, *Acinonyx rex*, commonly known as the king cheetah.

However, in 1981 wildlife conservationists at the DeWildt Cheetah Centre in South Africa bred a cheetah cub that had the markings of a king cheetah. Since both of the cub's parents were *Acinonyx jubatus* with the standard markings, biologists recognized that this was merely a rarely occurring variation and not a separate species.

by geography, that have some slightly different external features, such as coat patterns, but are still able to produce fertile offspring with members of other subspecies.) Other experts go one step further and classify the Asian form of the cheetah *Acinonyx venaticus* as a separate species from the African cheetah, *Acinonyx jubatus*. Many other experts believe that these differences in coat are not enough to justify such classification. They note that even between the two supposedly different species, individuals are more alike than, say, laboratory rats from the same litter.

Betting on speed

In terms of evolution, the *Acinonyx jubatus* that emerged over the eons followed the strategy of speed in its struggle for survival. Many physical characteristics of large cats, such as strength and bulk, were sacrificed in order for the cheetah to run down its prey more efficiently than any other animal on the planet. It was these drastic adaptations in favor of speed that caused the cheetah to evolve into a creature distinct from all other cats.

Virtually everything about the cheetah is in some way an adaptation for speed. For example, cheetahs grow to about the same length as leopards, generally around four feet and occasionally as long as fifty-three inches. But they are slightly taller at the shoulders and are much thinner than leopards. A cheetah's muscles are long and lean, and the animal has no significant fat reserves to slow it down. Even its head is smaller, its neck shorter, and its skull lighter and more delicate than those of other big cats. Adult cheetahs can weigh as little as 86 pounds (39 kilograms) and rarely top 140 pounds (64 kilograms).

The cheetah has an extremely flexible spine and loose joints that allow it to stretch out to a twenty-three-foot (seven-meter) stride when it runs. The upper vertebrae of the spine have an exceptionally long bone extension that provides an attachment for extra running muscles. A cheetah has long, thin legs and small, narrow paws. Unlike the other big cats, its claws are not fully retractable. They act something like spikes in track shoes and, along with the ridged toe pads, give the animal greater traction for maximum acceleration.

Cheetahs must meet the energy-guzzling requirements of high speed with a heart that is not well suited for pumping

Facts About Cheetahs

Scientific Classification: *Acinonyx jubatus*

Status: Endangered

Size
- 86–140 lbs. (39–64 kg.)
- 44–53 in. (112–135 cm.) head and body
- 26–33 in. (66–84 cm.) tail

Running Speed
- 70 miles (112 km.) per hour

Habitat and Range
- Flat grasslands, semidesert regions
- Africa and the Middle East

large quantities of blood. According to Bernhard Grzimek, "Like all other cats, the cheetah has a relatively small heart that pumps only a small amount of blood per heart beat."[1] Cheetahs compensate for this deficiency somewhat with a high concentration of oxygen in their blood. A distinct bulge in the front of the skull just above the eyes accommodates a large nasal passage that allows a greater flow of air into the animal's lungs. This efficient breathing apparatus allows cheetahs to supply more oxygen to their muscles with each heartbeat.

All of these features enable the cheetah to burst from a standing position to top speed in less than four seconds. Streaking over the ground at three strides per second, cheetahs have been accurately clocked at speeds approaching 70 miles (113 kilometers) per hour, by far the fastest speeds ever recorded for land animals.

Other features of a cheetah's anatomy are also adaptations for speed. The cheetah's blinding speed poses a maneuverability problem. Any creature traveling at the speeds that a cheetah attains could easily overrun a prey that changes direction suddenly. And just as an automobile can overturn when taking a corner at high speed, an animal trying to pursue an agile quarry could easily lose its balance. This problem is solved to a great extent by an exceptionally long tail (twenty-six to thirty-three inches, or sixty-six to eighty-four centimeters) that serves as a counterbalance and allows the cheetah to keep its balance when making the sudden changes of direction at high speed.

Sacrifices for speed

The cheetah's adaptations to maximize running speed have not come without a price. The animal's body plan has sacrificed strength in favor of speed. Cheetahs do not have the bulk and muscle that allow lions, tigers, and leopards to bring down larger prey. Likewise, the large nasal cavity that brings in extra oxygen for running leaves less room in the skull for teeth. Compared to other large cats, cheetahs have small, weak jaws and smaller teeth available for killing and eating their prey.

Similarly, although the cheetah's unretractable claws provide good traction needed for high-speed pursuit, they are at a disadvantage when it comes to climbing. Because they cannot be retracted, the claws are constantly exposed to hard surfaces. They quickly become worn and dull, like those of a dog. Therefore, cheetahs are not much better than dogs are at climbing, and this means that they cannot take refuge from danger in trees the way that leopards do.

Cheetahs also have less body fat than other large cats. This absence of fat reserves may make the cheetah lighter and faster, but it leaves the animal more vulnerable to hunger. Without fat reserves to fall back on, a cheetah has little margin for error in finding food. Unlike leopards, tigers, and lions, which can thrive by capturing one good-sized animal in a week, cheetahs cannot go more than a

Cheetahs developed long, thin bodies designed for speed and have much less fat and muscle than lions and tigers.

few days without making a kill. That can be a difficult problem if a cheetah suffers even a minor leg or foot injury. Entirely dependent on speed for hunting success, cheetahs may quickly starve to death if an injury hampers their running.

The evolutionary trade-offs that have allowed the cheetah to acquire its unmatched speed have left the entire species vulnerable to extinction. Cheetahs have never been a particularly abundant species even under the best of conditions. But until recently, the numbers of cheetahs in the world have held steady. It has been the explosive growth of another species, humans, that has provided the greater challenge to the cheetah's existence.

Cheetahs and humans in early history

The cheetah's speed and grace have won the admiration of humans from the earliest days of recorded history. There are documents dating back five thousand years that describe these animals being kept in captivity by wealthy rulers. Since cheetahs are more easily tamed than other big cats, they have been popular choices as mascots through the centuries. Many heads of state, from the pharaohs of ancient Egypt to the kings of Assyria to the great European emperor Charlemagne in the Middle Ages, liked to show off their power and majesty to visitors by having these stately beasts on leashes in their palaces.

In addition to rulers of nations, wealthy people have also kept cheetahs simply for the thrill of seeing the animals' spectacular running skills in action. In Egypt, the Middle East, and parts of Asia, hunters made a sport of sending their tamed cheetahs off to hunt antelope and deer. This type of activity reached its peak in India, where hunters enjoyed setting up displays of the

For centuries, humans used tame cheetahs to help them hunt.

greatest life-and-death races that nature has to offer. Blackbucks, which could reach speeds of fifty miles (eighty kilometers) per hour and zigzag with incredible agility, provided a challenge that only a cheetah could meet. Rulers frequently set their cheetahs after this prey in a location where they could watch the spectacle. The cheetah would be hooded until the prey was spotted. Then the hood was removed and the cheetah was released. When a cheetah succeeded in catching its quarry, it would give up the blackbuck to its master, who would reward his pet with a portion of the kill. During such hunts there was little chance of a cheetah escaping into the wild. Cheetahs tired quickly and were easily recaptured by riders on horseback if they tried to run away.

Some Indian rulers devoted enormous resources to their hobby. According to legend, a sixteenth-century Mogul emperor named Akbar the Great owned a thousand cheetahs for such hunting purposes.

Unfortunately, while cheetahs were easily tamed, keepers could not get them to breed in captivity. This meant that the stocks of "pet" cheetahs had to be continually replenished with new individuals captured in the wild. This put a constant drain on the wild populations.

Cheetahs in the twentieth century

Still, at the dawn of the twentieth century no one suspected that cheetahs would soon be battling for their very existence. Wildlife experts estimate that there were roughly one hundred thousand cheetahs roaming the wild at that time, and they were known to reproduce quickly in the wild. They seemed to prefer dry, semibarren areas that were less desirable regions for large human populations and so were largely left alone. Moreover, because of the coarseness of cheetah fur, cheetah pelts were not greatly in demand by the fashion industry, which meant that poaching of cheetahs was minimal.

Nonetheless, by the middle of the twentieth century cheetahs were in serious trouble. Human populations in regions where cheetahs lived grew at an ever increasing pace, forcing farmers, ranchers, and villagers into formerly unoccupied lands. This population growth encroached on the habitat of cheetahs as well as their prey. In India relentless hunting of cheetah prey further reduced the numbers of animals. Unable to find prey and restricted in their hunting territory, their numbers steadily shrank through the late nineteenth and early twentieth centuries. By 1952 there were no wild cheetahs remaining in India and Pakistan.

The story of cheetah decline repeated itself elsewhere in Asia and the Middle East. Wherever humans and cheetahs came in contact, the cheetah population gradually declined and then disappeared altogether. The last surviving cheetah in Saudi Arabia fell to a hunter's bullet in 1950. Within several years, the species disappeared in Jordan, Israel, and Syria.

At the close of the twentieth century, the cheetah vanished from Asia and the Middle East except for one small surviving population in the Khosk-Yeilagh Wildlife Reserve in the rugged mountains of northwestern Iran. There, an estimated two hundred cheetahs continued to roam, feeding primarily on wild sheep. Most experts believe that the only reason why this tiny population has survived is because the reserve is located in an area that is desolate and nearly inaccessible to humans.

African cheetahs

The cheetah has had better luck in Africa, but it is still in trouble there, too. The species at one time was found in most parts of the continent, except for the dense jungles along the equator and the wasteland of the Sahara Desert. Cheetahs especially thrived in the flat grasslands, where enormous flocks of gazelles, impalas, and other small hoofed animals provided a ready food source. As in Asia, the growth of human populations began to crowd the cheetahs and their prey out of some of their range. The human population of Africa, however, remained far less dense than that of Asia. Many African cheetahs were able to live undisturbed in drier, semidesert regions that humans avoided populating. Furthermore, many African nations recognized the unique value of their wildlife; as early as the 1940s, some of these nations set aside large game preserves where cheetahs, along with many other wild animals, were able to roam without human interference.

For a time, efforts to preserve the cheetah seemed to be working. As late as the 1970s, many experts on African wildlife declared that cheetah populations were in good shape and in no danger of extinction. This optimism, however, was soon shaken. Despite the efforts of some governments to maintain thriving animal populations, cheetah populations not only shrank but also began to do so at an alarming rate. Since the 1960s, cheetahs have disappeared from at least thirteen African countries in which they once thrived.

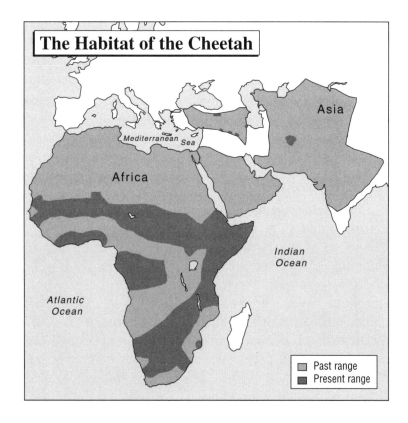

The Habitat of the Cheetah

The exact numbers of cheetahs in a particular area is difficult to determine. In Africa, wildlife-census workers try to determine the cheetah population by flying overhead in airplanes and counting the animals. This method has not been useful, though, because cheetahs are elusive and their roaming territory is quite large. Currently, the best estimates put the world cheetah population at fewer than fifteen thousand—perhaps even fewer than ten thousand—scattered throughout twenty-six African countries and Iran. In most of these countries, the populations are so small and widely scattered that experts do not expect the cheetahs to be able to find, mate with, and raise enough young to sustain the population for more than a few decades at best.

A species in peril

The bulk of the world's wild cheetah population is now confined to two areas. The largest stronghold is in the dry grasslands of Namibia in southwestern Africa, where approximately one fifth of all remaining wild cheetahs live. This region receives very little rainfall and so has not been farmed or occupied heavily by people. Despite finding prey more scarce here than on the fertile grasslands, cheetahs have been able to survive in this semidesert.

In recent times, however, Namibian ranchers have expanded their operations even into these last cheetah refuges. Although the land is too dry for the growing of many crops, it provides enough food for grazing animals. Experts now estimate that as many as 95 percent of the cheetahs in Africa live on land that is claimed by private livestock or game farmers. The outlook is grim, for whenever humans have been in direct competition with cheetahs for the land, cheetahs have always lost and eventually disappeared.

The other concentration of cheetahs is in the large game preserves that sprawl across southern Kenya and northern Tanzania. However, some experts have argued that cheetahs are not thriving even in those protected lands. While the game preserves have made cheetahs safe from human competition, they have put them in direct competition with other, more powerful predators, such as lions.

In addition to wild cheetahs, several hundred members of the species live in zoos throughout the world. Because they are easily tamed, cheetahs have usually adapted well to captivity. However, modern zoos have had only limited success at getting cheetahs to reproduce. The problem was compounded by the discovery in the early 1990s of a potentially dangerous virus that caused an immunodeficiency disease in captive cheetahs across the United States. Fearful that an outbreak of this disease could devastate the zoo populations of cheetahs, the American Zoo and Aquarium Association put a temporary ban on breeding until blood from every North American cheetah could be analyzed and screened for evidence of the virus.

The moratorium affected cheetahs adversely in a couple of ways. The average age of captive zoo cheetahs increased as no new cheetahs were born to take the place of the older ones. Furthermore, fertility among captive cheetahs decreased. When female cheetahs do not breed for a lengthy

A lion brings down a zebra. On game preserves, cheetahs must compete for prey with lions and other powerful predators.

period of time, their reproductive systems tend to shut down. This is what happened during the two-year moratorium on breeding from 1995 to 1997. In addition, age took its toll on fertility. "What has happened is a lot of these animals have aged to the point where they're past their reproductive prime," according to Randy Junge of the St. Louis Zoo. "All of a sudden, our cheetah annual reproduction has dropped off, at the same time our population has gotten older."[2]

Currently, the success rate in breeding captive cheetahs is so low that most zoo populations are not self-sustaining. Advances in captive breeding of cheetahs since 1985 have offered hope that populations of this species can be maintained. But the question of whether captive breeding will also be able to help sustain wild populations of cheetahs has not been answered.

The fate of the cheetah

It has become obvious to researchers and others that the cheetah cannot survive on its own in the modern world when it is forced into competition with humans and other species. Even the more optimistic observers understand that if future generations are to witness the breathtaking sight of a cheetah accelerating to top speed in pursuit of a gazelle, people are going to have to take steps to preserve the species.

2

Hunting on the African Plain

ENSURING THE SURVIVAL of the cheetah requires an understanding of exactly how the animal lives and what it requires for its existence. Primarily by studying cheetahs in the protected parks of Kenya and Tanzania, researchers have found out a great deal about their habitat needs, feeding habits, and threats to their existence, although many mysteries remain.

Animals of the plains

Cheetahs would not be able to use their speed well to capture prey if they had to weave through trees, plow through dense shrubs, or scramble up steep, rocky ridges. For this reason, they thrive only in open, relatively flat plains, where they can spot prey from a long way off, creep closer while hidden in grass, and then sprint unimpeded to catch their quarry. The small hoofed animals such as Thomson's gazelles, springbok, and impala that comprise the cheetah's main prey make similar use of the terrain. Like the cheetah, they are extremely fleet of foot and their best chance for survival is on the open plain, where they can see predators approach and can use their speed to escape.

The open, flat plains where cheetahs thrive occur only where rainfall is light and humidity is low. Cheetahs are well adapted to such dry conditions. They have been observed to go as long as ten days without water. Wildlife researchers have watched them repeatedly pass by water holes without stopping to drink even in the hottest weather.

Staking out territory

Like most members of the cat family, cheetahs are generally loners. Females, in particular, go out of their way to avoid any contact with their own kind, except for the litters that they are raising. Even immature cheetahs seem to develop an early hostility to any cheetahs unrelated to themselves. Upon reaching maturity, males go off to establish their own territory while females generally inhabit the territory used by their mothers. But even though they may share this territory for a number of years, mother and

Cheetahs are solitary animals and avoid contact with others of their species.

grown offspring have no contact with each other. On the rare occasions when they sight each other, they are careful to stay out of each other's way.

Males may restrict themselves to a territory of as little as fifteen square miles (thirty-nine square kilometers). The females' territory is much larger. They may travel over forty miles (sixty four kilometers) within their allotted area, covering an area of over three hundred square miles (roughly eight hundred square kilometers) as they follow the migrating gazelle herds. One reason for the disparity between the size of territory for males and females is that females often must supply food for several cubs as well as themselves and thus need a larger area in which to hunt. The large range required by females for their existence keeps the cheetah populations relatively sparse compared with other large cats. A wildlife researcher in Serengeti National Park, which straddles Kenya and Tanzania, noted, for example, that the average time required to locate a lion was seven minutes, but it took five hours to find a cheetah.

Leaving scents

Because a cheetah's living space may be large and occasionally overlaps with that of other cheetahs, some biologists have concluded that cheetahs are less territorial than other cats. Most experts, however, note that cheetahs establish the boundaries of their territory just as other cats do, by leaving their scent—in the form of urine—on rocks, trees, and other features of the land. As they roam across their territory, cheetahs sniff many of these same areas to determine if intruders have left their scents.

Furthermore, male cheetahs compete with each other for territory, and these encounters can be violent. As a result, most male cheetahs join forces with other males, usually littermates, to help them acquire and defend territory. About two-thirds of the males in Serengeti National Park live in pairs or trios. Some males never do acquire territory, however, and wander about as nomads. The difficulty of trying to avoid conflict with territorial males may cause them to roam hundred of miles from their birthplaces. The division of territory among members of the species is a primary reason why there are fewer male cheetahs than females in the wild. Forced to try and establish themselves in new territory that might not be as favorable as that in which they were raised, male cheetahs find survival even more difficult than females do.

 ## Cheetah Attack

Cheetahs are considered the tamest and most timid of the big cats. But the violence that competition for territory provokes even in such mild-mannered beasts has shocked observers with its intensity. Wildlife biologists George W. and Lory Herbison Frame once reported a savage encounter that occurred when a group of male cheetahs wandered into another group's domain.

The Frames had been observing one of the groups long enough that they identified the individuals by name. There were two brothers, whom the Frames called Tatu and Tano, who had joined with another male, Tisa, to establish and hold their territory.

When another group of three male cheetahs entered their territory, Tatu, Tano, and Tisa attacked. Two of the intruding males immediately retreated. The other one, however, made no move either to defend itself or to escape. He simply lay down while the three resident males attacked. The intruder's meek nature had no effect on its attackers, who savagely continued their assault. At one point, the resident males seemed worn out by their efforts and stopped to rest. Even then, the intruder made no attempt to flee. Eventually, Tatu, Tano, and Tisa returned to attack until they had killed the stranger. They then chased one of the other intruders for more than a kilometer (.7 miles), much farther than cheetahs normally run without resting.

The Frames' only explanation for the one intruder's refusal to defend itself was that it wanted to join the other cheetahs. They speculated that it submitted to the aggression in the futile hope that the attackers would understand that it was not contesting their territory and would therefore accept it into their group.

Hunting

Cheetahs can survive within their chosen territory only if they can find and kill prey on a regular basis. Because of their speed, cheetahs are able to kill prey more efficiently than any other of the large cats. Lions, for example, seldom succeed on more than one of every three or four hunts. Tigers, despite their tremendous strength, stealth, and leaping ability fail on at least nine out of ten hunting efforts. Cheetahs, in contrast, are able to capture their intended targets nearly half of the time. And when their target is a fawn or a hare, they almost always succeed.

One mother cheetah tracked by researchers in the Serengeti killed twenty-four gazelles and a hare in twenty-six days. Such a high success rate is crucial to the cheetah's survival. Unlike lions, which are powerful enough to bring down wildebeests, zebras, and water buffalo weighing over 1,000 pounds (approximately 450 kilograms), the

Because cheetahs are relatively lightly built, they hunt prey that weighs less than one hundred pounds.

Cheetahs and Hunting

- Prey: Thomson's gazelle, impalas, hares, and wildebeest calves.

- About one-half of cheetah hunts are successful.

- Cheetahs hunt by day.

- Cheetahs stalk their prey to within 30 yards (about 27 meters) before their chase.

- The average chase lasts about 15 to 20 seconds.

- Cheetahs learn to hunt at about 6 months.

lightly built cheetah has trouble killing animals that weigh over 100 pounds (45 kilograms). Cheetahs seldom work together to bring down larger prey, so they must kill far more often than other large cats to consume enough meat to survive. For example, whereas a lion may require only twenty to thirty kills in a year, a mother cheetah with a large brood of cubs cannot last more than a couple of days without making a kill.

Cheetahs are also unique among the larger cats because they hunt exclusively in broad daylight. They rely on eyesight, rather than smell, to locate prey, keep it in focus during the chase, and alert them to obstacles. This means that they need daylight to see where they are going, for even a cat's superior night vision cannot distinguish subtle changes in terrain while running at sixty miles (ninety-seven kilometers) per hour.

Cheetahs frequently hunt during the late morning and early afternoon hours, when more powerful predators such as lions are resting in the shade. Although they, too, prefer to sit out the heat of the noontime sun in the comfort of shade, cheetahs never pass up a kill if the opportunity arises. Even when they lie down to rest, they generally choose a spot that offers at least one good field of view. Occasionally they interrupt their naps to check if a prey animal has wandered within range.

A cheetah begins its hunt by scouting the terrain for prey. Cheetahs are proportionately taller than other large cats and have eyes located high on their heads so they can see a long distance. They often gain an even greater field of vision by perching on a termite mound, rock outcropping, low tree branch, or even the hood of a safari van.

Their preferred prey is the Thomson's gazelle. This animal weighs only about forty to sixty pounds (eighteen to twenty-seven kilograms) when full grown, and is thus small enough for a cheetah to subdue without difficulty. Quick enough to avoid most large predators, these gazelles roam the grasslands in enormous herds. Researchers have counted more than 180,000 in the Serengeti. But an animal that must kill every couple of days cannot afford to be choosy. When a Thomson's gazelle is not available, cheetahs will try for other small hoofed animals such as impalas and springbok. In Namibia, where Thomson's gazelles are rare, their primary prey is the kudu and the warthog. In Iran, where most of their traditional prey has vanished, cheetahs have adapted to living off wild sheep. African cheetahs will occasionally go after very young wildebeests, zebras, and even giraffes. Although they do not stalk hares, they easily catch them whenever they flush one out of the brush, and they have been known to eat game birds, aardvarks, jackals, and rats when very hungry.

The stalk

Although they can outrun any animal alive, cheetahs cannot maintain their speed for very long. They can sprint for only 300 to 600 yards (274 to 549 meters) before they retire in exhaustion. The 60- to 70-mile-per-hour (97- to 113-kilometer-per hour) burst for which they are famous lasts for only a few strides.

A Thomson's gazelle, which can accelerate quickly to speeds in excess of forty miles (sixty-four kilometers) per hour, has nothing to fear from a cheetah as long as it maintains a safe distance. Given a comfortable head start, it can elude the cheetah until the predator tires. A cheetah's only chance for a kill, therefore, is to creep within striking range before it is detected. Upon spotting its prey, a cheetah crouches low and advances slowly through the long grass. Its spotted coat blends in well with its surroundings, making it hard to see as it crawls and nearly impossible to detect when it stands still.

When a gazelle, alert for signs of danger, looks up, the cheetah freezes. It will not move again until the gazelle returns to its feeding. Often a gazelle will detect the cheetah's presence, either through smell, sight, or warning from other animals. This does not necessarily cause the cheetah to give up. It may remain stationary for a long time, as if waiting for the prey to forget about it.

Because of its speed, cheetahs have a much larger margin of error than other large cats. Even with the speediest gazelle, a cheetah needs only to approach to within thirty yards (about twenty-seven meters) to have a good chance

A cheetah crouches in the grass, stalking its prey and waiting for the right moment to attack.

of success. By comparison, a lion must get within ten yards (about nine meters) or so of most prey animals before pouncing in order to have a good chance at making a kill. It must surprise and capture the prey before it has a chance to accelerate to top speed.

The chase

Sometimes, in very open terrain, cheetahs will trot openly toward a large group of gazelles. In the confusion of the mass flight that this approach provokes, they may get close enough to a make a kill without stalking. But even when approaching a large herd, cheetahs never chase a group of prey animals; they always single out one victim. According to the *Encyclopedia of Mammals*, "Pursuing cheetahs have been known to run right past other prey individuals or race through the middle of fleeing herds without deviating from their chosen victim." [3] If they fail to catch that animal, they end the hunt rather than switching to a different individual.

As the chase begins, a cheetah chooses a single animal and focuses its efforts solely on that target.

The success of the hunt depends on the cheetah's judgment in selecting the right prey animal. In cases where the cheetah approaches a large herd, this means making an instant decision at the moment of attack. To avoid wasting time and energy in futile high-speed chases, it goes after animals that are easiest to catch and kill. This usually means young or very old animals or those that are paying the least attention.

When the cheetah charges its chosen target, the gazelle springs into action, accelerating, darting left and right, and making abrupt turns to elude its pursuer. This evasive action is sometimes enough to save the gazelle's life. With the balancing aid of its long tail, cheetahs are remarkably skilled in making the necessary high-speed adjustments to stay with the prey, but as in any high-speed chase, the slightest errors in calculation are greatly magnified. Observers have witnessed fast-closing cheetahs losing their balance when trying to react to a gazelle's move, especially on sloping or uneven ground, and taking a hard fall. If the cheetah is a split second off in matching any of the sharp turns of the gazelle, it loses ground, prolonging the chase. The gazelle needs only to elude the predator for a matter of fifteen to twenty seconds before the cheetah tires and gives up the chase.

Instinct over hunger

Ironically, a cheetah's instinct to chase its prey is so strong that it seems baffled by the rare cases in which a prey animal does not flee. Wildlife observers noted one case in which a gazelle had been severely wounded by a poacher. When charged by a cheetah, it struggled to gain its feet but was too weak to stand. Although the cheetah was hungry, it did not attack the animal. The cheetah lingered for an hour, waiting for the beast to flee, but the gazelle managed only to totter a few feet. Finally, the cheetah left the animal and went off in search of more conventional prey. Cheetahs have been seen similarly abandoning a hunt when a prey animal stands its ground.

Cheetahs make an exception to this rule, however, in the case of fawns. A baby Thomson's gazelle will often drop to the ground and hide, motionless, at the approach of a predator. Cheetahs appear to understand this behavior and will often conduct a thorough search of an area abandoned by gazelles in hopes of turning up a hidden fawn that was left behind when its elders fled.

The kill

Wildlife experts speculate that one reason for the cheetah's reluctance to attack a stationary animal has to do with a cheetah's killing technique. Cheetahs lack the strength and the lethal claws of other large cats. They are therefore unable to use the killing method of lions and tigers, namely, bringing down prey by pouncing on an animal and then gaining a firm grip with their sharp, curved claws and using their weight and strength to muscle the beast to the ground. Instead, cheetahs gain control of their prey with a swipe of their paw that trips the fleeing animal. They have a small claw on their forepaws, known as a dewclaw, that helps hook the hind legs of their victim to knock it off balance. Because it is very difficult to trip an animal that is standing still, cheetahs are likely reluctant to deal with stationary prey. Fawns are the exception because they are small and weak enough for a cheetah to overpower.

Like virtually all large cats, cheetahs kill by going for the throat. However, their teeth are not lethal enough for them to kill with a single, well-placed bite as lions and tigers often do. The cheetah clamps its jaws over the throat of the prey and suffocates it, taking care to avoid the flailing hooves. Again, a cheetah's jaws are not nearly as powerful as those of other large cats, so even an animal as small as a gazelle will occasionally wriggle out of the grip of the cheetah and make its escape.

The recovery

Cheetahs require an enormous amount of energy for their hunts. Their instant acceleration and furious sprint quickly leave their muscle cells starved for oxygen.

Unfortunately for cheetahs, their method of killing does not allow them to quickly replenish their oxygen

supply. They have to use their mouths for strangling their prey, which means that when they need air the most, they must go several minutes breathing only through their nostrils. Although cheetahs' expanded nasal passages allow them to take in more air through the nose than other cats, they are still extremely winded when they finish most kills.

A cheetah's jaws are not as strong as those of other large cats, and prey can sometimes escape.

Not only are cheetahs often exhausted after their high-speed chases, but they also frequently overheat, especially when hunting under the hot African sun. Many times they are unable to eat until they have had a chance to rest and cool down. Overheated cheetahs may have to breathe as often as three and a half times per second as they attempt to cool off. Sometimes they have enough energy left to drag their prey to a hiding place before they rest; other times they must take time to recover before they can hide the kill. During this period of recovery, which may last as long as a half hour, they are especially vulnerable to having their meal stolen by scavengers.

When cheetahs do eat, they do so quickly and nervously, frequently glancing around between bites. They can consume a huge amount of meat at a single feeding—up to a third of their own body weight. The cheetah's preference for huge meals makes it possible for observers to tell when it has last eaten by quickly glancing at the animal's stomach. Cheetahs do not save anything for future meals. Whatever they do not eat immediately upon killing, they leave for scavengers.

3

Reproduction and Development

LIKE ANY SPECIES, cheetahs can survive only if they possess an efficient means of replacing individuals that die. Wildlife biologists concerned with the survival of the cheetah have spent a great deal of time, both in the African wild and in zoos, studying how cheetahs mate, reproduce, raise their young, and mature into adulthood.

Mating

Since male and female cheetahs do not live together and rarely even associate with one another, sexual reproduction requires a special mechanism to ensure that pairs mate. In cheetahs, as in most large cats, the female's body generates certain hormones whenever it produces an egg and is ready to mate—a condition known as estrus. This can occur at any time of the year and generally lasts about two weeks. Male cheetahs can detect the presence of this hormone in the female's urine.

All cheetahs mark their territory with urine many times a day, but a female in estrus does so even more frequently. She typically leaves urine marks every ten minutes, and one female in the Serengeti was observed to deposit a scent mark twenty places in an hour. A male who comes across one of these markings immediately recognizes the close presence of a female that is ready to mate. Whereas he normally would avoid the female, in this case he follows the markings in search of her and

The Large Cat that Does Not Roar

One of the differences between cheetahs and other large cats of the Eastern Hemisphere is in their voice boxes. In lions, leopards, and tigers (as well as jaguars of the Western Hemisphere), the hyoid bone, which lies at the base of the tongue, has been replaced by a flexible piece of cartilage. It is the vibrations of this cartilage that produce the distinctive, resonating roar for which these cats are noted. Lions, in particular, can send out a roar that can be heard more than five miles (eight kilometers) away. Like all smaller cats, cheetahs have the normal hyoid bone.

The noises that cheetahs make are surprisingly soft and nonthreatening. Animal experts describe the mating call of cheetahs as a yelp or a bark. The sounds that mother cheetahs use to communicate with their cubs are often compared to the the chirping of a bird. When cheetahs are threatened and take a rare defensive stance instead of fleeing, they do not have the intimidating roar of the lion to help their cause. The best they can do is spit and hiss.

Lacking the ability to roar, a cheetah may spit or hiss.

calls out occasionally. The female answers the call and the two meet.

When the male and female cheetah meet, there are no elaborate courtship displays. The cheetahs seem torn between their natural avoidance of each other and the temporary attraction caused by the female being in estrus. The female appears to submit reluctantly to mating almost immediately, and then perhaps once more in the next twenty-four hours. After that, she shows no further interest in the male and tries to go her own way.

Males, however, are often reluctant to part. They keep a close eye on the female and follow her everywhere, refusing to sleep for fear that she might get away.

Wildlife observers have seen cases in which a male cheetah kept a female virtually captive for twenty-four hours before giving in to exhaustion. The minute the male fell asleep, the female ran off. Once the female gets away, the relationship is ended and the cheetahs go back to their solitary ways. The male has nothing to do with the offspring produced by the mating.

Cheetahs have a relatively short gestation period—that is, the time during which the cubs develop fully in the womb and are ready to be born. About three months after mating, the female gives birth to the cubs. Even this short pregnancy puts the mother at a survival risk, however, for an animal that relies exclusively on speed and agility to gain its food, the increased bulkiness in the final days of pregnancy makes hunting difficult. Starvation is therefore a very real danger for the expectant cheetah.

Baby cheetahs

The litter size for cheetahs is usually three to four cubs, although the number may be as few as one or as many as eight. There is no advantage to the cheetah that produces a large litter. A cheetah that gives birth to more than three or four cubs faces an enormous task in providing food for such a large brood. On the other hand, single cubs are also at a disadvantage. Experts observe that "it is common for mothers to abandon a lone cub rather than invest time in its survival."[4]

Cheetah cubs are tiny, weighing only between 5 and 10 ounces (approximately 150 to 300 grams) at birth. Their coats do not resemble that of adult cheetahs. Instead of the tawny coat with black spots, they have long, woolly, dirty white hair (called a mantle) that runs along their backs and is a smoky gray below. At three months, they lose their baby coats and the characteristic spots begin to appear.

Some biologists believe that this unusual coat is a survival adaptation. Baby cheetahs are utterly helpless and are easy prey for any predator who happens upon them. They are not able to open their eyes for the first week or so, cannot stand until about nine days, and are unable to crawl, much less walk, for the first three weeks. During this most vulnerable period, their light-on-top, dark-underneath birth coats resemble that of the honey badger, a tough, aggressive little animal with sharp claws that most predators avoid. The baby cheetah's coat may help it survive by fooling predators into thinking that it is a honey badger and should be left alone.

While cheetahs are normally timid and flee at the first sign of danger, the mother may undergo a dramatic personality change when cubs are involved. Observers reported one case in which a lioness approached a mother cheetah and her two cubs. The mother growled a warning. Fright-

The typical litter size for a mother cheetah is three or four cubs.

Cheetahs and Reproduction and Development

- Sexual maturity: 20 to 23 months

- Gestation period: 90 to 95 days

- Average litter size: 3 cubs

- Average weight of newborn cubs: 5.25 to 10.5oz. (150 to 300g)

- Number of cubs that survive to adulthood: Less than one-third

- Longevity: Up to 19 years in captivity. An estimated 12 to 14 years in the wild

---

ened out of their wits, the cubs fled. But, having no idea of what they were supposed to be running from, they ran straight toward the lioness.

The mother cheetah salvaged a disastrous situation by outsprinting the cubs to the lioness and swatting it with her forepaw. The lioness was so stunned by the cheetah's aggression that she instinctively retreated. The cheetah chased her for about ten yards (nine meters) while the cubs scattered and dove for cover in the grass. Wildlife observers also report cases in which the mother has purposely lured lions into chasing her in order to lead them away from her cubs.

Little nomads

Mother cheetahs are not able to offer their cubs much protection from the weather. Unlike other cats, they do not build a nest or burrow into the shelter of a rocky den. The best they can do is hide the newborn cubs in tall grass, patches of dense vegetation when it is available, or under bushes among rocks. When heavy rains or hail pour down on the plains, there is nothing to prevent the young cheetahs from getting soaked or battered. Under such circumstances, some

Young cheetahs may be left alone for long periods of time as the mother hunts or moves her cubs one at a time to a new lair.

cheetah cubs fall victim to the elements. During much of the time that the young are in the lair, they are alone. Although very young cubs feed on their mother's milk, the mother must continue to hunt to provide for her own needs. As a result, cheetah mothers have been known to leave their young alone for as long as forty-eight hours at a stretch. In addition, there are occasions when the mother simply appears exhausted by the constant demands of the cubs and goes off by herself for a brief time to recover.

A young cheetah never lives in any single lair for very long. Every few days, and in some cases every day, the mother moves the cubs to a different spot. For example, wildlife researchers watched one mother cheetah relocate to ten different lairs in fifteen days. The frequent moves are necessary, however, because if the cubs stayed in one spot, they would build up a concentration of odors that could attract predators. When her cubs are too young to crawl or walk, the mother picks them up one at a time by the scruff of the neck and carries them to the new spot.

Sometimes the new lair is far away. Other times it may be as close as fifteen feet (five meters) and may offer no more shelter than the abandoned one. After carrying the last cub to the new location, the mother often returns to the original lair and searches briefly, as if checking to make sure she has not lost count and left one behind.

This constant moving continues after the cubs are able to walk by themselves. After the first five or six weeks, the cubs are weaned from their mother's milk and require meat. They follow their mothers around and begin eating from her kills. Since the cubs are not yet strong enough to travel long distances, the mother gradually moves the lair closer to the prime hunting grounds. The bright white tip of the mother's tail serves as a marker to help the young keep sight of her as she walks through the tall grass. The cubs constantly chirp whenever the mother is out of sight to maintain contact with her, and she sometimes chirps back to help them locate her. Occasionally, a cub falls so far behind that the mother has to go back and look for it.

Despite the constant movement, mothers rarely lose their cubs. According to George Frame, "Experience with mothers and their cubs showed me that mother cheetahs are not likely to lose their cubs through carelessness or stupidity. They have well-developed maternal behavior and they seem intelligent and persistent." [5]

Wildlife observers once followed a mother as she led her cubs on a journey of over five miles (eight kilometers). Cheetah cubs may not all develop at the same rate, and in this case four of the cubs were able to keep up with the mother but one fell far behind. After reaching her destination, the mother returned three miles to the straggler, then carried and led the cub back to join the rest. In another instance, a mother cheetah searched three days for a cub that apparently had been killed by a predator in her absence.

The importance of play

A cheetah cub's preparation for adult roles begins early. Before cheetah cubs can even walk, they are already biting, kicking, and batting at each other in the lair. Play is the cubs' training program for honing the muscles and reflexes they will need later in life, and they spend much of their waking hours in some form of physical interaction.

Cheetah cub frolicking is different from that of lions and tigers and reflects the differences in their methods of hunting. Lion and tiger cubs do a great deal of wrestling, an exercise that helps them develop the strength they require for bringing down prey. Although young cheetahs occasionally wrestle, most of their play involves adult cheetah hunting skills, such as stalking, ambushing, pouncing, and chasing, and swatting at each other's hind legs. They frequently chase birds, although they seldom catch one. When they grow older, cheetahs may further exercise their running and maneuvering skills by teasing other animals. Even rhinoceroses sometimes find themselves pestered by young cheetahs, who are fast enough to easily escape the animals' frustrated responses.

The mother cheetah is not spared from this activity. Young cheetahs playfully attack her as they follow her from place to place. Cheetah mothers are exceptionally patient with this roughhousing; they do their best to ignore it, and they never strike back.

There are times when the cubs' play actually poses a danger to the family's survival. At about six months, the cubs chase after the mother as she attempts to stalk her prey. They spoil hunt after hunt with their noisy activity, forcing the mother to spend even more of her time trying to find food.

Learning to hunt

Also at about this age, the cubs begin a long and often awkward transition from simply eating what their mother kills to capturing their own food. When mothers capture relatively helpless prey, such as a rabbit or fawn, they often bring it still alive to the cubs and release it so that they may practice their hunting skills.

Researcher Joy Adamson observed the behavior of a litter of cubs when the mother first presented them with a still-living baby gazelle. At first the cubs appeared con-

fused as to what they were supposed to do. They flinched and retreated whenever the wounded gazelle kicked, trying to gain its feet.

If the captured prey is healthy enough to run, the young cheetahs instinctively chase after it. They swipe at it with their paws, trying to knock it down. If they succeed, they grab hold of the prey's throat with their jaws in the classic cheetah killing technique.

Young cheetahs sometimes fail to bring down even small fawns, and they often have trouble hanging on or applying enough pressure to suffocate the animal. If the gazelle escapes from them, the mother repeatedly recaptures it and brings it back to the cubs for another try. She will intervene and make the kill herself only if the cubs appear overmatched by the prey they are trying to bring down.

Just as learning to make a kill can be a lengthy matter of trial and error, the skills required for stalking and bringing down prey also require a great deal of practice. Young

Play is vital to cheetah cubs' survival, developing muscles and reflexes that they will later use when they hunt.

cheetahs usually show poor judgment in their first hunting attempts. Some of their most frequent mistakes include going after animals that are too large and strong, carelessly giving away their presence as they make their approach, and starting their sprint too soon.

While the young cheetahs are learning to hunt, they pose an enormous burden to the mother. As they grow larger they require much more food, yet they are not able to make their own kills. At the same time, their bungling attempts to hunt often spoil good hunting opportunities for the mother.

Breaking away

The cubs stay with their mother until they are nearly full grown. In most cases, they go off on their own at around sixteen months, although it can be as soon as eleven months and as late as twenty. Unlike a cheetah's gradual introduction to hunting, the parting of ways occurs suddenly and without any evident preparation. Wildlife experts have yet to under-

A mother cheetah assists her cub in pursuing its prey.

Why No Family Togetherness?

Wildlife experts have a number of speculations as to why cheetahs show such indifference to their own flesh and blood. One explanation is that the easy severing of family ties helps cheetahs disperse so that they are not all competing for food in the same territory.

Some wildlife biologists suggest that cheetahs must also necessarily separate themselves from other cheetahs because their style of hunting is best suited to solo work. Gazelles would be more apt to detect a cheetah's presence if several of them were in the area instead of one. However, since there is no reason why cheetahs could not live together and hunt either individually or cooperatively, not every expert is convinced by these explanations.

A more likely explanation of why cheetahs shun family ties is that their inability to defend their kills from scavengers makes them a marked target on the grasslands. Whereas single cheetahs may escape notice, a group of them is more easily spotted and therefore would be more likely to attract scavengers looking for an easy meal.

stand what triggers the split. One observer saw a mother and her two fifteen-month-old cubs resting together as usual one October evening. By the next afternoon, the cubs and the mother had separated permanently. The observer saw no behavior prior to the separation that differed in any way from behavior the cheetahs had displayed all along.

This sudden breakup of the family contrasts with the behavior of other large cats. For example, when leopard offspring are ready to go off on their own, they begin by making a series of short solo expeditions. Upon returning from these trips, they greet other family members with enthusiastic affection. Only after several experiences of being out on their own do the leopards sever ties with the mother for good. From the instant of their first separation, however, a cheetah mother and her cubs act as though they are complete strangers.

Interestingly, while retaining no attachment to the mother, cheetahs show some bonding with their siblings. Littermates leave the mother as a group and tend to remain together for several months. Females always pull away one by one and live on their own eventually, but male littermates often stay together for life. This behavior contrasts with that of other large cats. Among lions, for example, females stay together under the direction of a dominant male, and the young males go off separately in search of new territory.

The breakaway period can be a difficult time for young cheetahs. Most of them have not yet become skilled hunters. If they cannot catch a meal for themselves every two to five days, they will starve.

Continuing the reproductive cycle

Cheetahs reach sexual maturity very quickly for a mammal of their size. A two-year-old female may give birth to a litter of her own. She may continue to produce a new litter every year of her life, which averages about twelve to fourteen years in the wild. Cheetahs have lived as long as nineteen years in captivity and are still capable of reproducing at age fifteen.

The ability to produce a large number of offspring might be expected to give cheetahs a survival advantage over less prolific large predators. Increasingly, however, experts question whether that advantage is enough to ensure the survival of the species in a highly competitive and rapidly changing world.

4

Natural Competition

ONE OF THE factors that endangers cheetah populations is the harsh reality of competition. In nature, many creatures compete for the same resources. Those creatures that find themselves overmatched by other species must either adapt to a new lifestyle that avoids direct competition with those species or they will eventually become extinct.

The experts agree that survival has always been a struggle for the cheetah. According to the *Encyclopedia of Mammals*, "It appears that, long before the human influence on the species precipitated its decline, the cheetah was a rather naturally scarce, low-density animal, living quite close to the edge."[6] For although the cheetah is remarkably adapted to catching small, swift animals such as gazelles, these adaptations have left it vulnerable to competitors in other areas.

The threat of scavengers

Unfortunately for cheetahs, catching and killing a prey animal is only half the battle. Because they are built for speed and not strength, they are not well equipped to defend their kills from other predators. Their high-speed chases often leave them too exhausted and overheated to defend themselves even against relatively small scavengers. Likewise their feet are adapted for sprinting and not climbing, so they are unable to stash their kills in trees where less nimble animals cannot get them, as leopards do, for example.

Furthermore, cheetahs are not aggressive by nature. Their usual reaction when they see a lion or leopard is to meekly slink away, head low. When any animal approaches them directly, they almost always immediately run away, even from animals that are not physically a threat.

All carnivores of the plains are aware of these weaknesses, and they keep a close watch for cheetahs. Hyenas and jackals follow cheetahs in hopes of snatching a freshly killed meal from them. A researcher who followed a single cheetah for several weeks observed that three of her twenty-five kills were stolen by other predators. Typical of the cheetah's plight is the case of a female whom researchers observed ambushing and capturing a Thomson's gazelle that wandered too close to her. But before she had even finished suffocating her prey, a hyena charged at her. The cheetah immediately let go of the gazelle and retreated. The hyena snatched the dazed gazelle before it could start running, and carried it away.

Cheetahs rest in the shade and watch their kill being eaten by jackals. After the hunt, cheetahs are often too hot and tired to defend their kill from scavengers.

Lions and hyenas are the most frequent thieves of cheetah kills, but leopards and baboons will also move in when
the opportunity arises. Cheetahs immediately abandon
their kill to these animals without a fight and with only the
mildest sign of irritation. Jackals, warthogs, and even vul-
tures have been observed to drive a tired cheetah away
from its kill with little, if any, resistance.

Working hard for survival

Unlike their rivals on the plains, cheetahs do not scav-
enge meat killed by other animals. They acquire every
meal by hunting, and they expend a great deal of energy to
capture it. Frequently, the enormous effort that cheetahs
expend in a hunt goes to waste when scavengers take what
the cheetah has earned. In contrast, rival predators such as
lions spend most of their time resting and storing up energy. When they take a cheetah's kill, they acquire food
with virtually no effort.

The cheetah's disadvantage in this food-gathering system is one of the factors that puts the animal's survival at
risk in the modern world. According to the *Encyclopedia
of Mammals,* "The cheetah seems to work harder for its
living than do other big cats of Africa, and thus may be
more vulnerable to environmental changes brought about
by human disturbance."[7]

Genetic diversity

A great deal of scientific debate in recent years has cen-
tered on findings that cheetah populations have almost no
genetic diversity. Genetic diversity refers to the amount of
variation in the genetic makeup of individual members of
the particular species.

In the early 1980s studies by molecular biologists
found that there is less genetic variation among cheetahs
than in any other mammal. In fact, totally unrelated cheetahs from different areas of Africa are more alike genetically than most human brothers and sisters are. One
measure of this lack of diversity was the fact that cheetahs easily accepted skin grafts from totally unrelated

The cheetah population has very little genetic diversity, a fact that threatens their survival.

cheetahs. Normally, an individual's immune system is different enough from other species members that it will consider transplants from them as an infection. Cheetahs, however, were so similar that their immune systems could not tell the difference between their own skin and a transplanted section of skin from an unrelated cheetah.

Why so little diversity?

Many biologists believe that the cheetah's lack of genetic diversity can be traced back about ten thousand years. According to this theory, climatic changes known as the Ice Age wiped out most of the cheetahs in the world. The species was barely able to survive and repopulate from a small group of survivors who were closely related. With no influx of different genes from other populations, the gene pool has remained stagnant.

Some experts believe that the cheetah's highly specialized adaptations have added to the problem because they leave no room for genetic diversity. Bernhard Grzimek expresses a commonly held view when he says, "It may be that a system reduced to such a one-sided high-level performance—as the cheetah is to speed—simply cannot tolerate even the slightest deviation to the norm." [8]

Threat to survival?

Some scientists have argued that this absence of diversity poses a serious threat to the cheetah's survival as a species. Genetic variation provides protection from deadly diseases and sudden changes in the environment. For example, if a new disease strikes a genetically diverse population, the odds are good that some individuals' immune systems will be better equipped to cope with the new threat. Animals with these immune characteristics will tend to survive. They will pass those characteristics on to future generations, who will then be well equipped to fight off the disease.

A population with little genetic diversity, on the other hand, is at great risk from deadly new diseases. In the case of the cheetah, scientists worry that virtually the entire population could be vulnerable to a single disease. The concern is real. Some scientists note that a large number of captive cheetahs have been plagued with immunodeficiency viruses and with diseases of the liver, kidneys, and central nervous system.

Just as a genetically diverse population is less vulnerable to disease, so too is such a population better equipped to cope with a dramatic environmental or habitat change. Where there is no genetic diversity, if one member of the species is not equipped to survive the change, the odds are that none will.

Effect of inbreeding on reproduction

Farmers have known for centuries that inbred livestock (those whose parents came from the same family and so have little genetic variation) tend to produce fewer healthy offspring than livestock that are not inbred. In 1978 experiments at the National Zoological Park in

Washington, D.C., showed that the same tends to hold true for inbred zoo animals.

Most zoos have had no better luck than the Indian rulers of past centuries in getting captive cheetahs to produce healthy offspring. Even the zoos with the most successful captive-breeding programs have failed to achieve enough reproduction among cheetahs to maintain their numbers. Of the 266 cheetahs living in North American zoos, only

Tourists photograph cheetahs in a zoo. Cheetahs in zoos produce very few offspring, despite the efforts of captive-breeding programs.

26 males and 27 females were able to become parents of cubs between 1987 and 1991. Only 18 percent of captive cheetahs have ever bred at all, and only 6 percent have borne more than one litter.

Why captive breeding has limited results has been a source of controversy. Noting the cheetah's striking lack of genetic diversity, many animal experts concluded that the problem was caused by inbreeding. Biologists cited cheetahs as the prime example of the dangers of inbreeding to a population's survival.

Many zoos then looked into ways to increase genetic diversity among their cheetah populations. They hired geneticists to determine the genetic makeup of their animals and made a great effort to mate unrelated animals. When possible, they attempted to mate individuals from different parts of the world.

Causes of infertility

In the late 1980s and early 1990s, however, researchers began looking more closely at the causes of these infertility problems. David Wildt and his colleagues from the National Zoo traveled from zoo to zoo to determine whether the inability of many cheetahs to breed could be positively linked with inbreeding. Among their findings was the fact that over 75 percent of all sperm produced by cheetahs in zoos was abnormal. Furthermore, wild cheetahs were found to have an unusually high abnormal sperm count. Since abnormal sperm is one of the common results of inbreeding, this finding appeared to establish the link between inbreading and infertility.

But on detailed examination, Wildt was surprised to find that sperm counts in cheetahs varied greatly from zoo to zoo. He also found that, in many places, those cheetahs who were able to breed had about the same sperm count and other reproductive characteristics as those that did not breed. Furthermore, one study of wild cheetahs revealed that nineteen out of twenty cheetahs were easily able to reproduce despite the fact that they showed no more genetic variation than those in captivity. Researchers, in fact,

Some experts believe that cheetah cubs have a high mortality rate because the lack of genetic diversity leaves them prone to birth defects.

could find no physical reason why captive cheetahs should have less success at breeding than wild ones.

The studies produced no evidence that genetic diversity had any effect on the ability of cheetahs to conceive and bear offspring. Most researchers concluded that care of the animals, and not inbreeding, was the major factor in the failure to breed cheetahs in captivity. As Oliver Ryder, a geneticist at the Zoological Society of San Diego, says, "The simplest explanation is we don't know how to breed cheetahs well."[9] For example, even the most experienced handlers had difficulty trying to determine when a female cheetah was in estrus.

Inbreeding and juvenile mortality

The effect of inbreeding on how well cheetah cubs survive has similarly been debated. Inbreeding, or lack of genetic variation, could be a factor threatening the cheetah population if it caused females to give birth to cubs with birth defects that reduced their chance of survival. In fact, juvenile mortality has traditionally been high in cheetah cubs bred in captivity. The combination of high mortality and the lack of genetic variation led many to suspect that inbreeding was causing the high mortality.

Donald Lindburg of the Zoological Society of San Diego studied juvenile mortality among cheetahs to see if this was so. He found that cheetah cubs survived as well as other cubs in similar situations, and few of the infant deaths could be traced to genetic defects. Studies of cheetah litters in the wild also found few cub deaths that could be blamed on genetic defects. Lindburg argues that, again, ignorance of the proper way to care for them, and not inbreeding, was the main cause of infant mortality in captive cheetahs.

The debate continues

There remains uncertainty about how seriously the lack of genetic diversity threatens the survival of the cheetah. Jonathan Ballou, a population biologist at the National Zoo, admits, "It's possible for populations to do quite well without genetic diversity, at least on the short term." But he insists that "we certainly have enough data to say that, in general, the lack of gene diversity puts a population at risk."[10] Most zoos therefore continue to keep their cheetah populations small as a precaution against large-scale loss of the animals to epidemics.

Other experts, however, argue that there is no evidence that inbreeding has caused any wild population to decline. "The effects of inbreeding and loss of genetic diversity on the persistence of populations in the real world are increasingly questionable,"[11] writes T. M. Caro and M. Karen Laurenson.

Juvenile mortality

Zoologists worry that the debate over the effects of genetic diversity has caused people to overlook or downplay more important threats to the cheetah's existence. The experts point out that the vast majority of cheetah deaths in the wild are due to nongenetic juvenile mortality.

M. Karen Laurenson studied cheetah cubs in the Serengeti. By placing radio collars on females, she was able to locate

The Florida Panther—A Hint of What Lies Ahead?

As cheetah populations dwindle, wildlife experts begin to compare their plight to that of the Florida panther. The Florida panther is a population of mountain lion that adapted to the swamp, grass prairie, and palm, oak, and cypress wetlands of southern Florida.

The Florida panther has undergone a drastic decline in the past century. Its numbers are believed to be confined to large wetlands known as the Everglades. It has been protected by law since 1958. The federal government has joined Florida in spending millions of dollars to purchase land to preserve as wildlife habitat, on research in the wild and in the laboratory, on medical treatment and vaccinations for the animals, and for building tunnels under highways to give the panthers access to more habitat.

None of this has helped much in rebuilding the Florida panther's numbers. Although the task of counting such secretive animals in over 2,300 square miles (nearly six thousand square kilometers) of impassable Everglades wetlands is nearly impossible, experts believe that only thirty to fifty of the animals remain. Many experts believe that inbreeding among so small a population is an insurmountable obstacle to the panther's recovery. The Florida panther's reproductive rate has been so severely reduced that its extinction is all but inevitable without human intervention. Wildlife experts are fearful that the cheetah is approaching this same point of no return.

The Florida panther is on the brink of extinction.

their lairs. While the females were away on hunts, she entered the lairs to count and weigh their newborn cubs. She kept tabs on all of the families and noted that by the time the cubs were old enough to leave the lair (about two months), only 36 of the 125 cubs (29 percent) were still alive. Only 6 of the cubs (5 percent) survived to full maturity. Other researchers have noted even higher mortality rates. In their two-year study of cheetahs, Karl and Katherine Amman did not see one cheetah cub that survived to adulthood.

Only about 10 to 20 percent of cheetah cubs survive into adulthood.

While some zoologists believe that these reports exaggerate the death rate, even the most optimistic concede that at least 80 to 90 percent of cheetah cubs in the wild never reach adulthood. This compares with a 50 percent death rate among the young of other cats in the wild.

By far the greatest threat to young cheetahs is predators. Lions and hyenas kill an estimated 75 percent of cheetah cubs. Hyenas prey on the cubs as a source of food. Lions do not eat cheetahs, but they will kill and leave any that they find, as if instinctively bent on eliminating any possible competitors for prey. Adult cheetahs are too fast for lions to catch, unless they are injured or ambushed; but the young are easy victims. If smaller predators such as jackals and even birds of prey find a cheetah lair while the mother is away on a hunt, they, too, can make a meal of the helpless cubs.

Adult mortality

Kevin Crooks, a researcher at the University of California at Santa Cruz, wanted scientific data to identify the key factor in holding down cheetah populations in the wild. He came up with a computer model that could predict what would happen to a cheetah population under a wide variety of conditions. Using his program, Crooks looked at different rates of reproduction and survival, life spans, and numbers of predation.

When he ran all of these variables through the program, he concluded that, in most situations, the survival rate of the adults and not the cubs had by far the most effect on population growth. This was due to the cheetah's rapid rate of reproduction. Even when a female loses an entire litter, she can produce a new litter within a year. Over the span of the cheetah's twelve- to twenty-four-year life, she could easily produce forty cubs. That meant that she could raise the two cheetahs necessary to maintain the population even with a juvenile mortality rate of 95 percent.

Crooks's study did not examine the factors that influenced the survival of adult cheetahs, however. The fact remains that, even during its most prosperous times, the cheetah has never been an abundant species. Whether due to disease, scavengers, predation, hunger, inbreeding, or any other factor, the margin of survival for cheetahs has always been slim. That left them particularly vulnerable when humans placed ever-increasing stress on them by drastically altering their environment.

5

Human Causes of Cheetah Decline

ACCORDING TO T. M. CARO and M. Karen Laurenson, "There is widespread agreement that the environmental consequences of human distribution present the greatest challenge to most populations in the wild."[12] In other words, the many species that are disappearing in nature are doing so because humans have been crowding them out.

Human population explosion and animal habitat

In the past few centuries, humans have become the most successful species in the history of Earth as far as dispersing into various habitats and dominating them. In the 1830s the human population reached 1 billion for the first time. That figure doubled over the next hundred years, reaching 2 billion in the 1930s. The rate of population growth continued to accelerate so that within just fifty years, the population doubled again to 4 billion. Although population growth has slowed and even stopped in many of the more affluent areas of the world, the human population has continued to expand, reaching 6 billion by 1999. The greatest rate of growth continues to take place in Africa, home of many large mammals, including the cheetah.

Unlike other species, humans are capable of completely reshaping their environment in response to their needs or wishes. As the human population grows, the destruction of natural habitats to support humans grows as well. People with high standards of living consume enormous amounts of natural resources. Fields, forests, and wetlands are plowed up and paved over to provide housing, factories, stores, and entertainment for the masses. People in impoverished nations, locked in a desperate struggle for day-to-day survival, do not have the luxury of looking ahead to the future consequences of their actions. They must try to feed their families by farming land that had previously been left in its natural condition.

Loss of habitat

All of this expansion and altering of the environment has come at the expense of animals. Human encroachment has

Destruction of wilderness by humans has threatened many species of animals, including the cheetah.

taken land to which many species were uniquely adapted and has made it uninhabitable for them.

Loss of trees and the destruction of ground cover in the cultivation of land has led to massive erosion. Billions of tons of topsoil have been blown away by the wind or have been washed out into the oceans. This has left the land less suitable for agriculture or any other form of life. The term *desertification* describes the process of turning livable habitat into desert wasteland through poor conservation techniques. When this fragile land is exhausted the demand grows for even more land to be converted to farms.

Every acre of habitat devoured by a city, converted to desert, plowed under by farms, and fenced off as pasture, has squeezed the wild animals onto an ever-shrinking resource base. Even those animals that have not been directly affected by human encroachment are harmed when the prey animals on which they depend for their existence dwindle in number.

Surveying the effects of this erosion of habitat to human expansion, the Cheetah Conservation Fund concludes, "The cheetah has suffered a devastating decline of available habitat and prey."[13] The cheetah has been exceptionally hard hit by this loss of habitat because of its way of life. Since cheetahs require a larger hunting territory than most predators, they suffer more acutely than most creatures when their habitat is carved up for human development. Since they require abundant game in order to live, the decline in prey has been disastrous. Because even stable cheetah populations are relatively sparse and have limited success in raising a large number of their young to adulthood, cheetahs cannot recover quickly from sudden population losses caused by habitat destruction.

Conflict with farmers and ranchers

Agricultural expansion has forced cheetahs into a deadly confrontation with an enemy they cannot defeat. Like many animals harmed by habitat destruction, many chee-

Livestock ranches in Namibia, such as this sheep farm, alter the natural environment and drive out the cheetah's prey.

tah populations had been able to survive in past decades only by moving onto lands poorly suited for human agriculture and habitation. Until recently, this unused and unwanted land provided them with a relative haven from human interference.

In the closing decades of the twentieth century, farmers and ranchers moved onto much of this previously vacant land. In Namibia, which has more cheetahs than any other country in the world, the number of ranchers who raise cattle and sheep has risen to more than twenty-five hundred. In Kenya, wheat farmers trying to raise enough food to keep up with the country's exploding population growth have encroached on cheetah domains. Farmers destroy the native vegetation that feeds the animals on which the cheetah preys. Ranchers also bring in livestock, which alters or destroys the natural ground cover, and they fence in vast areas that had been open to free-ranging animals. These drastic changes in the environment have driven out or reduced the cheetah's natural prey.

Given a choice, cheetahs prefer to hunt wild prey rather than livestock. Cheetahs are not large enough to pose a danger to adult cattle. And, because they are so timid, they do not attack even goats and sheep in areas where the flocks are closely tended. There is no such thing as a man-eating cheetah—a single unarmed human can almost always frighten them away. But when prey is scarce and cheetahs go hungry, they will not pass up an opportunity to kill a sheep, goat, or an unprotected calf. Because many of the new ranches are on relatively barren land, they must encompass an enormous area to provide enough food for the livestock; and in such cases, vulnerable livestock are likely to go untended.

On the rare occasions when cheetahs kill livestock, they draw the wrath of farmers and ranchers. In recent years they have gained an unfair reputation as a marauder of livestock. Laurie Marker, head of the Cheetah Conservation Fund, notes, "Even though other predators such as hyenas, jackals, and leopards also eat the ranchers' livestock, the cheetah gets the blame. That is because it hunts during the day when people are more likely to see it."[14] Leopards, for example, often escape notice because they hunt at night. They are so adept at staying out of sight that they often live near populated areas without humans ever being aware of their presence. In the very driest areas of its range, the cheetah may get blamed for kills made by the caracal, a slightly smaller desert cat.

The war on cheetahs

Some ranchers have set up enterprises that put them in direct conflict with cheetahs. In an attempt to attract the business of foreigners wanting to hunt African game, they have established "game camps," where they raise exotic animals on private land and charge visitors for the privilege of hunting them. Unfortunately, cheetahs take advantage of these game camps, where their natural prey present them with an irresistible source of food.

Faced with what they view as a threat to their livelihood, farmers in southern Africa have persecuted cheetahs with a vengeance. Farmers and ranchers find that they can catch cheetahs rather easily, especially the younger ones, in cage-like traps. Worse, even in areas where cheetahs are protected, farmers hunting on their own property can get permission to shoot livestock-killing cheetahs. In many

Cheetahs are not difficult to trap, and farmers and ranchers often do so to protect their livestock.

cases, farmers and ranchers kill the cheetahs whether or not they have permits.

The hostility of farmers towards cheetahs runs so deep that some farmers are totally unmoved at the thought of cheetahs going extinct in the wild. Upon encountering a wildlife advocate working to preserve cheetahs, an embittered farmer recently growled a warning: "Don't forget that a whole bunch of people don't like you or your cheetahs!"[15]

A few uncompromising farmers or ranchers can wreak havoc on a threatened species. Between 1980 and 1991, at least sixty-eight hundred cheetahs, more than a third of all wild cheetahs in existence, were shot or sold off to zoos by Namibian ranchers. In one year, two farmers were responsible for the elimination of thirty-nine cheetahs in Namibia, more than a fourth of all cheetahs captured or killed in the country that year. Added together, the legal and illegal killing of cheetahs has depleted the world's population of wild cheetahs.

The high demand in the 1960s for fur from spotted cats contributed to the decline in cheetah populations.

Hunting and poaching

Farmers and ranchers are not the only people who have taken up arms against cheetahs. For centuries, sport hunters have stalked and killed both cheetahs and the prey on which they depend for their survival. In most countries, shooting cheetahs for sport is illegal. Yet, despite the dwindling number of cheetahs in the world, some countries continue to offer a limited number of permits for cheetah hunting. In 1997 eighty-seven cheetahs were killed by trophy hunters, primarily in southern Africa. Some hunting groups have been lobbying African governments for increased availability of cheetah-hunting permits.

There are also people who hunt cheetahs illegally. Although cheetah fur is not as prized as some other cat fur because of its coarseness, during the 1960s the high demand for spotted cat fur in fashion put cheetahs at risk. Many hunters risked breaking the law to earn the high bounties that such furs could command. They even penetrated the supposedly protected national parks and game refuges to collect their animals. From 1968–1969, more than three thousand cheetah pelts were imported into the United States alone. Thousands more ended up in Europe and Japan.

Most of these cheetahs were killed illegally. However, authorities found it virtually impossible to prosecute anyone for this crime. Different countries had different rules regarding cheetahs. Since there was no way of proving where and under what rules the cheetah was taken, governments had great difficulty trying to prosecute and convict anyone of poaching.

In the 1970s society reacted strongly against killing large cats for fashion purposes, and the trade in cheetah fur has virtually stopped. Presently, the cheetah is protected on public land in most of the countries in which it still lives. But again, such hunting has taken a greater toll on cheetahs than on many other species because of the narrow margins by which cheetah populations survive in the wild. Whenever people have reduced cheetah populations by hunting,

Extinction of the Cheetah in India

The most dramatic demonstration of the effect that human activities can have on cheetahs occurred in India in the late nineteenth and early twentieth centuries. The cheetah's preferred prey was the blackbuck, which had flourished so well over the centuries that it had become the most abundant hoofed mammal in the region. The beautiful blackbuck was prized by hunters for its striking colors; long, graceful corkscrew horns; and its flavorful meat. As the population of hunters grew, they killed the blackbucks by the hundreds of thousands.

The effect of the slaughter was compounded when increasing demand for food and living space forced farmlands to expand from the most fertile areas of India and Pakistan into some of the dry grasslands where the blackbuck thrived. When the native grasses were replaced by grain fields, the blackbucks were deprived of their source of food. They had no choice but to eat the farmers' grain. When farmers saw these animals destroying their fields, they regarded them as nuisances and shot them on sight. The result was mass extermination. An estimated 4 million blackbucks roamed India in the nineteenth century. By 1947 only an estimated 80,000 remained. Within a few decades, most of these were gone. The 8,000 or so that remained were either pushed into the driest desert regions or were confined to game refuges.

When farms took over the natural grasslands and caused the drastic decline of animals such as the blackbuck, the cheetahs of India were doomed. Unable to find prey and to establish their hunting territory, their numbers steadily shrank. By 1952 there were no wild cheetahs remaining in India and Pakistan.

A blackbuck.

poaching, trapping, or removing them from the wild for zoos or a personal collection, the species has had difficulty returning to its previous population levels.

Even more devastating than the actual hunting of cheetahs has been hunting of cheetah prey. Hunting by humans wiped out the gazelles of Arabia in the late 1940s, and the extinction of cheetahs in that area followed swiftly. The near extermination of the blackbuck by hunters and farmers in India likewise spelled doom for cheetahs in Asia.

Problems with game preserves

Large game preserves such as the Serengeti National Park in Kenya and Tanzania offer the wide expanse of habitat that animals such as the cheetah require. They also protect the animals from humans by banning hunting within their boundaries. On the surface, therefore, these would seem like ideal safe havens for threatened species such as the cheetah.

Cheetah numbers, however, are not large even in game refuges that appear to offer ideal habitat and almost unlimited prey. This is partly because cheetahs, with their need for large hunting territory, exist in naturally low-density populations. But some cheetah experts point out that these supposed havens for wildlife actually present some new dangers. One of the most glaring problems is that the game reserves also provide protection for the cheetah's competitors. While a refuge such as Serengeti National Park, which covers thousands of square miles, may seem like a free and open habitat, it nonetheless confines cheetahs to living in a relatively small area alongside lions and other natural enemies. Cheetahs are unable to compete directly against lions; thus, wherever lion populations increase, cheetah populations decrease. The high population density of lions and hyenas in such parks puts cheetah cubs at enormous risk. It also increases the chances that a cheetah will lose its kill to a scavenger.

Even the largest of the game parks is an artificial system. Because these parks have boundaries put in place by humans that restrict the natural flow of species entering and leaving, they are not complete ecosystems. Wildlife experts warn that the interrelationships between the hundreds and thousands of species that make up an ecosystem are extremely complex. No one can possibly know how the establishment of park boundaries affects all of these interrelationships. The result is that game parks may produce an entirely different environment from that to which wild animals of that area were adapted. The effects of such artificially established ecosystems can be so hidden and wide-ranging that they are not understood until it is too late to undo the damage they have done.

A cheetah calmly walks in front of a truckload of tourists on an animal-watching safari in Africa.

Tourists and cheetahs

Another problem is that large game preserves also attract hordes of curious tourists. Many of these tourists have traveled thousands of miles and spent a great deal of money for the chance to see African animals in the wild. Tour guides realize that their livelihood depends on letting their customers see the animals they came to see. Some of them accomplish this with little regard for the welfare of the animals.

In places such as Serengeti National Park, cheetahs have adapted for the most part to the prying human presence. They often accept cars, vans, and buses as part of their habitat. They even take advantage of parked vehicles by resting in their shade, playing under them, and climbing atop them to get a good vantage point for scouting prey.

In many cases, however, the tourists' desire to see the fastest animal in the world in full sprint causes a hardship for these animals. Tour buses go out into the park at the cheetah's prime hunting times of midmorning and late afternoon. When a cheetah begins stalking a gazelle, a tour bus will often drive in close hoping for a good view of the kill. Oftentimes, the bus will alert the prey to the cheetah's presence. Other times the cheetah is so distracted by the interruption that it breaks off the hunt. Either way, the hunt is ruined.

There have also been cases of tourists deliberately chasing cheetahs in their vehicles, trying to provoke the animals into a race. Some cheetahs have been so bothered by tourists that they now hunt at noon—the hottest time of the day—so they can have an undisturbed hunt while tourists are back at camp.

Despite the fact that cheetahs suffer from harassment by tourists and that even in parks the cheetah's numbers are relatively small, some wildlife researchers believe that cheetah populations in these reserves are actually at or near the maximum natural density. These researchers contend that cheetahs are not a threatened species within those parks. Some believe that game preserves are the only safe havens. "Only in the vast designated preserves such as the Serengeti National Park can the cheetah hope to survive,"[16] say George W. and Lory Herbison Frames.

6

Efforts to Save the Cheetah

GUARANTEEING THE SURVIVAL of the cheetah is a large and complex task that requires the combined efforts of nonprofit organizations, governments, and individuals. Wildlife experts have identified several steps that must be taken if cheetahs are to continue to roam in the wild, including improvement of breeding, elimination of poaching, protection of habitat, protection of the cheetah's wild prey, cooperation with farmers and ranchers to improve livestock management, and education of the public.

Breeding cheetahs in captivity

If wildlife specialists could learn to breed cheetahs in large numbers in captivity, this could have at least two positive effects on cheetah survival. First, it would provide a ready source of cheetahs to replace those specimens that die in zoos, thus eliminating the need or desire to remove cheetahs from dwindling wild populations.

Secondly, captive-bred cubs could be shielded from the shockingly high predation rates that they face in the wild and could then be released when they are able to fend for themselves. In the absence of predators, cheetahs would be capable of rebuilding their numbers dramatically. They produce an average of nearly four cubs per litter and are physically ready to have another litter

The Cheetah Conservation Fund

The most determined group seeking the preservation of cheetahs is the Cheetah Conservation Fund. "There are only 12,000 cheetahs left in the world, and our goal is to save this species from extinction," says the organization's founder, Laurie Marker, in *CCF Newsletter #12*.

Marker grew up in Rolling Hills, California, with a dream of being a wildlife manager. Her dream came true when she got a job at Wildlife Safari Park in Oregon, working with cheetahs bred in captivity. She worked there for sixteen years, during which time she came in contact with Daniel Krause, whose area of expertise was big cats. The two married and pooled their talents and interests by moving to Washington, D.C., in 1988 to serve as codirectors of a research center that specialized in endangered species. While on the job, they became frustrated with sitting in an office, detached from the creatures that needed their help. "Why sit in Washington and talk about cheetahs?" Krause remembers thinking. "We have to be in Namibia to talk about cheetahs."

The couple moved to a remote area of Namibia with the immediate goal of educating Namibian farmers and ranchers about cheetahs, but they quickly realized that there was an arrogance in that approach. After all, they knew nothing about the land or the life that the farmers and ranchers were leading. Before they could expect to be taken seriously, they had to educate themselves. For months they drove across the arid, semibarren plains of Namibia, asking questions and observing the problems between cheetahs and private landowners.

In the course of less than a decade, the Cheetah Conservation Fund gained the confidence of government, school officials, and private individuals to emerge as the primary force working to protect the species. Laurie Marker continues to guide the efforts of the organization from her Namibia headquarters, although a large chunk of her time is taken up with travel and lectures to help raise awareness for her group.

within a year. If captive breeding of cheetahs were successful and carried out on a large scale, therefore, great numbers of cheetahs could be raised and reintroduced into the wild.

One large problem with this plan has been that cheetahs have always been extremely difficult to breed, although some zoos have made progress by paying greater attention to the cheetah's lifestyle. Many unsuccessful zoos had tried to put one cheetah male in a living situation with one female, ignoring the fact that males tend to live in pairs and that the sexes do not live together. Zoos that housed cheetahs in large "cat houses" next to other large cats had little success in breeding cheetahs. Given the fact that cheetahs are deathly afraid of lions, it was not surprising that they showed behavior far different from wild cheetahs. When cheetahs in zoos were separated from lions

By mimicking the cheetah's natural environment more accurately, some zoos have had increasing success with captive-breeding programs.

and taken out of permanent living situations with other cheetahs, their reproductive rates increased.

Nowhere has captive cheetah breeding been more successful than at the DeWildt Cheetah Centre in the foothills west of the the South African capital of Pretoria. The center traces its beginnings to 1968, when Ann van Dyke received a phone call from a farmer. Knowing that van Dyke had a special interest in caring for animals, he asked if she would take in two cheetah cubs that he had found. Contact with this threatened species inspired her, three years later, to use her family's wilderness acreage to create a research facility dedicated to breeding endangered species.

At first the DeWildt Cheetah Centre experienced the usual frustrations in trying to breed cheetahs. For years, their efforts ended in nothing but heartbreaking stillbirths. But the dedication of their staff of wildlife researchers eventually paid off with the center's first live birth in 1975. Since then, more than five hundred cubs have been born on the DeWildt grounds.

Under the guidance of highly trained wildlife biologists, zoos such as the San Diego Wild Animal Park have also made progress in breeding captive cheetahs. In 1999 the park announced the births of five cheetahs, its first births since 1994. Barbara Durrant, a reproductive physiologist at the park, is optimistic about the state of captive breeding of cheetahs. "It will only take one generation of new cubs to start the whole process again and get the breeding back up," says Durrant. "I think the cheetah population is secure."[17]

Restocking

One of the hopes of cheetah breeders is that cheetahs born in captivity can be transported to the wild to bolster wild cheetah populations or to reintroduce the species to areas in which it has become extinct. The DeWildt Cheetah Centre has made some explorations in this area.

The difficulty with this is that cheetah cubs depend on their mothers to teach them the skills and behavior needed to survive in the wild. Those born and raised in captivity have no role models or teachers to help them build on their instinctive behaviors. Likewise, they will get no cooperation from other cheetahs, who see them as unwelcome competition. Furthermore, cheetah cubs grow attached to humans and become dependent on them to meet their needs. The chances of such animals surviving in the wild against fierce competition is slim.

George W. Frame sums up the opinion of many conservationists when he says, "The captive breeding of endangered species (particularly carnivorous mammals), unless carried out in isolation from humans, will seldom result in successful reintroductions to the wild."[18]

Other concerns

Wildlife biologists have other concerns about reintroducing cheetahs to areas in which they once thrived but no longer do so. They point out that there was a reason why cheetahs were unable to survive in such regions. Merely putting more cheetahs in place will not establish a thriving cheetah population unless the original reasons for the cheetah decline are determined and addressed. So far, attempts that have been made to reintroduce cheetahs in South Africa and Kazakhstan have not been successful.

Experts are not convinced that reintroduction should be done even if it is possible. They note that humans have greatly altered many habitats in which cheetahs used to live. No one knows exactly how cheetahs would adapt to the new conditions. Newly released cheetahs may find it difficult to hunt their preferred prey and may become a nuisance by killing livestock. This could harm the reputation of all cheetahs and thwart attempts to get farmers and ranchers to leave them alone.

Furthermore, researchers such as Kevin Crooks argue that keeping adult cheetahs alive is far more crucial to maintaining cheetah populations in the wild than breeding cubs successfully in captivity. Crooks and others note that all the time, energy, and money spent on breeding cubs would be better used to safeguard adult animals struggling to cope with difficult conditions.

Raising Cheetahs as Pets

For thousands of years, people have known that cheetahs are far more comfortable around humans than most large cats are. The fact that they are easily tamed has probably saved the lives of many baby cheetahs, who frequently stumble into ranchers' and farmers' traps. Individuals such as David and Carol Cawthra Hopcraft have taken in these lost, injured, or unwanted cheetahs and nursed them back to health.

The Hopcrafts own a ranch near Athi Plains in Kenya. They had no particular interest in cheetahs until a man seeking work with them in 1980 brought with him a lost cub that he had found. The Hopcrafts took it in and raised it. They thought that was a once-in-a-lifetime experience until a veterinarian contacted them in 1992. He had nursed to health a cheetah cub that had been brought to him in a severely weakened state. Having heard that the Hopcrafts had experience raising a cheetah, he wondered if they would take in this one, too. Two years later the Hopcrafts happened across an abandoned cub on their own.

Cheetahs are by nature meek and docile, and they often seek affection from their human masters. This may lull their caretakers into thinking of them as totally harmless. They can, however, be provoked. When David Hopcraft ignored the warning growls of one cheetah and continued to grab at her food, the cheetah slashed him across the arm. The Hopcrafts children also learned not to make fast movements around the cheetahs—to be calm and firm. Carol Hopcraft, in an interview with *Life* magazine's Gina Kopecky, noted the contradictions of living with a wild animal: "When she's with us, she purrs, she's affectionate, she's absolutely part of our family," said Carol about one of her cheetahs. "But she's also wild. I can't tell you how it works but it does." Although the Hopcrafts allowed the cheetahs to roam free during the day, they shut them in at night to prevent confrontations with the growing human population in the area.

Government protection

Wildlife experts agree that the main priority in protecting threatened species such as the cheetah is preserving habitat. This is an area of conservation that is difficult to achieve, however, because it puts animals in direct conflict with people. "For the short run," observes a Tanzanian official, "if animals are to survive, people will have to make some sacrifices."[19]

It is often difficult to persuade individuals to make personal sacrifices for a cause such as animal preservation. Because growing human populations and economic needs place so much pressure on wildlife habitat, this issue requires the help of government.

The governments of African nations such as Tanzania and Namibia are concerned with preserving their wildlife heritage. The Namibian government has shown interest in establishing their country as the cheetah capital of the world. It has worked with private groups to develop some of the most detailed and advanced predatory conservation programs in the world. Tanzania and Kenya devote a much greater percentage of their land than most nations to wildlife habitat. "You will note that we call our department the Ministry of Wildlife and Tourism, not the Ministry of Tourism and Wildlife," says a Tanzanian wildlife official. "You see where our priorities lie." [20]

As their populations grow, however, and as they struggle to maintain a decent standard of living for their people, these governments face difficult choices about land use.

One area of wildlife conservation that governments have been able to control more successfully is the hunting of animals. Most countries now have strict regulations that outlaw the hunting of cheetahs. South Africa, however, has continued to allow a limited number of cheetah-hunting permits. Moreover, other countries have not been able to enforce existing laws against poachers and the killing of cheetahs by ranchers.

The government of Zimbabwe is considering relaxing its ban to permit safari hunting of cheetahs on private land.

Its reasoning is that foreign hunters would pay large sums of money to landowners for the privilege of shooting African big game. If farmers and ranchers are given this profit motive to maintain a cheetah population, they will stop killing the animals indiscriminately and instead invest time and money in protecting them as they might any other profitable resource. Critics of this plan argue that allowing any hunting of cheetahs would be a disaster because of the difficulty of monitoring such activity. Opponents of legalized hunting worry that poachers could simply claim that they obtained their skins legally on privately owned land.

Tracking and counting cheetahs

However wildlife advocates ultimately go about saving the cheetah, they will need to develop improved means of documenting the numbers and behaviors of cheetahs. Because of their sparse distribution and timidity, cheetahs have always been difficult to locate and count. As a substi-

Cheetah Conservation Fund director Laurie Marker (left) examines a cheetah before tagging it.

tute for largely ineffective counts conducted from airplanes, the Cheetah Conservation Fund's staff and volunteers have joined with Namibia's National Carnivore Monitoring Project to tag and monitor as many cheetahs as possible.

With the cooperation of ranchers and farmers, these groups began a program in 1998 of capturing and then putting radio collars on cheetahs. The collars serve two purposes. Researchers can immediately tell if an animal they catch has already been tagged, preventing that individual from being counted twice. Secondly, the radio collars allow researchers to track the cheetah's movements. The Cheetah Conservation Fund's Laurie Marker hopes to use this information to show ranchers that cheetahs usually just cross their land without bothering their livestock.

Protecting livestock and cheetahs

Wildlife advocates concede that under current conditions of reduced habitat and scarcer prey, cheetahs do kill livestock, especially sheep, goats, and very young cattle. They realize that they will have difficulty persuading farmers to stop trapping and killing cheetahs unless they find ways to reduce or eliminate that problem. As Marker says, "Our problem is finding ways that cheetahs can live with humans."[21]

One of the Cheetah Conservation Fund's most successful efforts in this area has been its guard-dog program. Since cheetahs are frightened off by any aggressive animal, trained dogs can easily protect vulnerable livestock from cheetahs. One of the best dogs for this purpose is the Anatolian shepherd. This ancient breed has been used in Turkey for more than six thousand years to protect livestock from predators. When the pups are very young, shepherds raise them with a flock of sheep. The dogs come to think of the flock as their own family. When danger threatens the flock, the dogs bark to warn away the intruder, and if that does not work, they will attack. The Cheetah Conservation Fund has not only urged private landowners to

Many ranchers use Anatolian shepherds to protect their livestock from cheetahs.

use dogs for livestock protection but has also bred and placed dozens of Anatolian shepherds with farmers and ranchers.

A few farmers have taken the innovative step of raising baboons, which are natural enemies of the cheetah, with their flocks. In addition to frightening away cheetahs, baboons also eat parasites that live on goats and sheep.

The Cheetah Conservation Fund has also been involved in conditioned taste-aversion trials. Volunteers mix a salt into livestock meat and feed it to cheetahs. The salt makes the cheetahs sick to their stomachs. The hope is that this unpleasant experience will discourage the cheetahs from killing and eating livestock.

Education

One of the main goals of the Cheetah Conservation Fund has been to reduce the alarming slaughter of cheetahs in Namibia by farmers and ranchers. In order to do this, the fund has to convince skeptical landowners that cheetahs are not the destructive animals that many take them to be. As farmers discover that cheetahs are not dangerous marauders and learn that dogs are effective in warding off the occasional raid, they no longer resort to killing them.

This education process has shown great gains during the 1990s. Arthur Bagot-Smith owns a 32,500-acre cattle ranch in Namibia. He once believed that he had no choice but to kill cheetahs to protect his herd. But after discussions with experts, he came to understand that these animals were not as harmful as he thought. Now he is an enthusiastic supporter of cheetah protection programs. "It's a question of adapting farmers to fit in with the cheetah,"[22] he says.

Another young Namibian farmer changed his mind about cheetahs after listening to Laurie Marker speak. When he heard that his neighbor had just caught a mother and her three four-month-old cubs, he gave his neighbor a horse in exchange for the cheetahs. Then he called the Cheetah Conservation Fund to come and take custody of the cats.

When a cheetah is brought to the Cheetah Conservation Fund's facility, volunteers usually measure the animal and take a blood sample for research purposes. Then they tag

Cheetah Conservation Fund volunteers care for a sick cheetah.

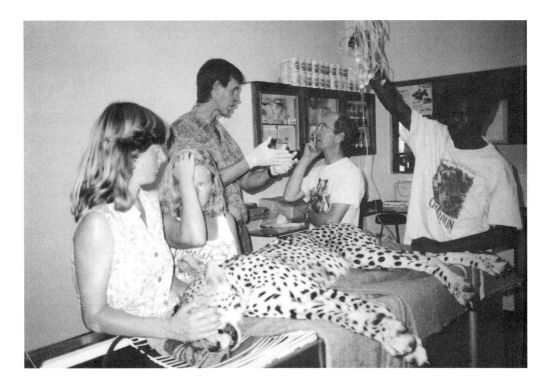

the cheetah so that they will know if this particular animal is caught again. Finally, they discuss the options with the landowner. If they can persuade the landowner that the cheetah is not likely to hurt his or her livestock, the cheetah is let go near where it was captured. If not, the animal is taken to a different location. Either way, the cheetah is returned quickly to the wild, especially if it is young, before it can become accustomed to human care.

Changing attitudes

Old attitudes are often the most difficult to change, so the Cheetah Conservation Fund is determined to bring its case to the younger generation of Namibians in the classroom. This effort has yielded some positive results. One twelve-year-old Namibian boy listened to a program about cheetahs at school. A short while later, his father trapped a cheetah on

U.S. zoo educators teach a class of children about cheetahs and how they are being threatened by extinction.

his farm and was about to kill it. But when the boy repeated to his father what he had learned about cheetahs in school, the farmer called the Cheetah Conservation Fund instead. As a reward for their actions, the Cheetah Conservation Fund gave the family an Anatolian shepherd.

Overall, the process of educating farmers and ranchers has proved enormously successful. While a few holdouts continue to view the cheetah as a menace to be killed on sight, the number of cheetahs killed by farmers and ranchers in Namibia has dropped drastically from several hundred each year to fewer than 150 in 1997. Wildlife conservationists are coordinating efforts to promote networking among various African countries so that farmers in Namibia can share the knowledge they have gained about cheetahs with their counterparts in places such as Kenya and South Africa.

The future

Much research is needed before an accurate prediction can be made about the cheetah's survival chances. The experts do not even have solid agreement about the numbers of cheetahs remaining in the wild. There are those who say that the cheetah's existence in game refuges is threatened, and those who say that the population, though sparse, is holding its own. Some experts believe that the cheetah's lack of genetic diversity indicates that it cannot survive long; others believe it is not a problem.

The diminishing habitat of the cheetah leads many to suspect that the only cheetahs that will remain in the twenty-first century are those in zoos, private game refuges, and national parks. In the words of George W. and Lory Herbison Frame, "Cheetahs today are outnumbered by their enemies, they are largely defenseless, and, where unprotected, they are likely headed for extinction."[23] The cheetah's survival in the wild depends on whether people will care enough to take the steps needed to protect it. Its fate rests largely in the hands of farmers and ranchers in Namibia and the few other locations where this fastest of all creatures still roams.

Notes

Chapter 1: Decline of the Cheetah

1. Bernhard Grzimek, *Grzimek's Encyclopedia of Mammals,* vol. 3. New York: McGraw-Hill, 1990, p. 584.

2. Quoted in Kim Peterson, "Hope for a Speedy Recovery," *San Diego Union-Tribune*, October 20, 1999, p. E-4.

Chapter 2: Hunting on the African Plain

3. *Encyclopedia of Mammals,* vol. 4. New York: Marshall Cavendish, 1997, p. 459.

Chapter 3: Reproduction and Development

4. Peterson, "Hope for a Speedy Recovery," p. E-4.

5. George Frame, *Swift and Enduring.* New York: E. P. Dutton, 1981, p. 70.

Chapter 4: Natural Competition

6. *Encyclopedia of Mammals,* p. 456.

7. *Encyclopedia of Mammals,* p. 461.

8. Grzimek, *Grzimek's Encyclopedia of Mammals,* p. 589.

9. Quoted in Elizabeth Pennisi, "Cheetah Countdown," *Science News,* September 23, 1993, p. 201.

10. Quoted in Pennisi, "Cheetah Countdown," p. 200.

11. T. M. Caro and M. Karen Laurenson, "Ecological Genetic Factors in Conservation: A Cautionary Tale," *Science,* January 28, 1994, p. 485.

Chapter 5: Human Causes of Cheetah Decline

12. Caro and Laurenson, "Ecological Genetic Factors in Conservation," p. 486.

13. Cheetah Conservation Fund, *Newsletter #12*, July 1999, www.cheetah.org.

14. Quoted in *Ranger Rick,* "New Chance for Cheetahs," September 1998, p. 16.

15. Quoted in Cheetah Conservation Fund.

16. George W. and Lory Herbison Frame, "Cheetahs in a Race for Survival," *National Geographic,* May 1980, p. 728.

Chapter 6: Efforts to Save the Cheetah

17. Quoted in Peterson, "Hope for a Speedy Recovery," p. E-4.

18. Frame, *Swift and Enduring*, p. 230.

19. Quoted in Frame, *Swift and Enduring*, p. 227.

20. Quoted in Frame, *Swift and Enduring*, p. 227.

21. Quoted in *Ranger Rick,* "New Chance for Cheetahs," p. 17.

22. Quoted in Susan Reid, "Cheetah's Champions," *People Weekly,* June 14, 1993, p. 134.

23. Frame, "Cheetahs in a Race for Survival," p. 712.

Organizations to Contact

American Zoo and Aquarium Association (AZA)
8403 Colesville Rd., Suite 710
Silver Spring, MD 20910
(301) 562-0888 • fax: (301) 907-2980
website: www.aza.org • e-mail: membership@aza.org

AZA represents over 160 zoos and aquariums in North America. The association provides information on captive breeding of endangered species, conservation education, natural history, and wildlife legislation. AZA publications include conservation and science publications, the *AZA Annual Report*, and *Communique,* a monthly magazine. Publications are available from the Publications Department at the address listed above.

Cheetah Conservation Fund (CCF)
WILD/CCF Program Director
PO Box 1380
Ojai, CA 93024
(805) 640-0390 • fax: (805) 640-0230
website: www.cheetah.org • e-mail: info@cheetah.org

The CCF is an organization dedicated to preserving the cheetah species. In addition to on-site troubleshooting and habitat preservation in Namibia, the organization is involved in research, education, and fund raising efforts to improve quality of life and survival chances for cheetahs.

Endangered Species Coalition (ESC)
1101 14th St. NW, Suite 1200
Washington, DC 20003
(202) 682-9400 • fax: (202) 682-1331
website: www.stopextinction.org • e-mail: esc@stopextinction.org

The coalition is composed of conservation, professional, and animal welfare groups that work to extend the Endangered Species Act and to ensure its enforcement. ESC encourages public activism through grassroots organizations, direct lobbying, and letter-writing and telephone campaigns. Its publications include the book *The Endangered Species Act: A Commitment Worth Keeping*, and articles, fact sheets, position papers, and bill summaries regarding the Endangered Species Act.

Foundation for Research on Economics and the Environment (FREE)
945 Technology Blvd., Suite 101F
Bozeman, MT 59718
(406) 585-1776 • fax: (406) 585-3000
website: www.free-eco.org • e-mail: free@mcn.net

FREE is a research and education foundation committed to freedom, environmental quality, and economic progress. The foundation works to reform environmental policy by using the principles of private property rights, the free market, and the rule of law. FREE publishes the quarterly newsletter *FREE Perspectives on Economics and the Environment,* and produces a biweekly syndicated op-ed column.

Hornocker Wildlife Institute
PO Box 3246
University of Idaho
Moscow, ID 83845
(208) 885-6871 • fax: (208) 885-2999
website: www.hwi.org • e-mail: hwi@hwi.org

Founded by Dr. Maurice Hornocker, the Hornocker Wildlife Institute conducts long-term research on threatened species and sensitive ecological systems. Through observation and exploration a framework is provided for satisfying a universal curiosity about the nature of wildlife and the effects of humans on the natural environment. The institute is a world leader in carnivore research and continues to work on these important indicators of ecological health. It is also broadening its focus through ongoing studies of whooping cranes and trumpeter swans, steelhead and salmon, wilderness vegetation succession, and wildlife populations in Latin America. In addition, it continues to press ahead in integrating good science and broad-based ecosystem approaches with cultural and economic factors.

IUCN/SSC Cat Specialist Group
Attn: Peter Jackson, Chairman
1172 Bougy
Switzerland
+41-21-808-6012
website: http://lynx.uio.no/catfolk • e-mail: pjackson@iprolink.ch

The Cat Specialist Group is an international panel of over 170 scientists, wildlife managers, and other specialists from forty countries who have volunteered their expertise to the Species Survival Commission of IUCN—the World Conservation Union, which is based in Switzerland. Its function is to provide IUCN, CITES (Convention on International Trade in Endangered Species), and governmental and nongovernmental organizations with advice on all matters concerning wild cats, including their status in nature, the threats they face, conservation requirements, and biology and natural history. The group publishes the newsletter *Cat News* to its members.

National Wildlife Federation (NWF)
8925 Leesburg Pike
Vienna, VA 22184
(703) 790-4000
website: www.nwf.org

The National Wildlife Federation offers environmental education programs in communities, in the outdoors, and in the classroom. Publications include: *National Wildlife* and *International Wildlife*, bimonthly magazines serving to educate readers about national and global conservation issues; *Ecodemia*, a book regarding campus environmental stewardship at the turn of the twenty-first century; *Conservation Directory*, featuring descriptions and contact information for over three thousand environmental organizations and government agencies; and *NWF Special Reports*, which are on-line environmental reports.

PERC

502 South 19th Ave.
Bozeman, MT 59715
(406) 587-9591 • fax: (406) 586-7555
website: www.perc.org • e-mail: perc@perc.org

PERC (The Political Economy Research Center) is a nationally recognized institute located in Bozeman, Montana. The primary goal is to provide market solutions to environmental problems. PERC pioneered the approach known as free market environmentalism. It is based on the following tenets: Private property rights encourage stewardship of resources; government subsidies often degrade the environment; market incentives spur individuals to conserve resources and protect environmental quality; polluters should be liable for the harm they cause others. Activities include research and policy analysis, outreach through conferences, books and articles, and environmental education at all levels. Publications include the quarterly newsletter *PERC Reports*, books by PERC authors and editors, and the Policy Series featuring short papers that apply the principles of property rights and markets to natural resource issues.

United Nations Environment Programme (UNEP)

Attn: Mr. Tore J. Brevik, Chief of Information and Public Affairs
PO Box 30552
Nairobi, Kenya
+254-2-62-1234/3292 • fax: +254-2-62-3927/3692
website: www.unep.ch • e-mail: ipainfo@unep.org

UNEP studies ecosystems, encourages environmental management and planning, and helps developing countries deal with their environmental problems. UNEP's publications include environmental briefs, the bimonthly magazine *Our Planet*, and numerous books available through its publications catalogue.

U.S. Fish and Wildlife Service

1849 C St. NW
Washington, DC 20240
(202) 208-3100
website: www.fws.gov • e-mail: web_reply@fws.gov

The U.S. Fish and Wildlife Service is a network of regional offices, national wildlife refuges, research and development centers, national fish hatcheries, and wildlife law enforcement agencies. The service's primary goal is to conserve, protect, and enhance fish and wildlife and their habitats. It publishes an endangered species list as well as fact sheets, pamphlets, and information on the Endangered Species Act.

World Wildlife Fund (WWF)
1250 24th St. NW
PO Box 97180
Washington, DC 20077-7180
(800) CALL-WWF
website: www.worldwildlife.org

WWF is dedicated to protecting the world's wildlife and wildlands. The largest privately supported international conservation organization in the world, WWF directs its conservation efforts toward three global goals: protecting endangered spaces, saving endangered species, and addressing global threats. From working to save the giant panda, tiger, and rhino to helping establish and manage parks and reserves worldwide, WWF has been a conservation leader for more than thirty-eight years. WWF publishes an endangered species list, the bimonthly newsletter *Focus*, and a variety of books on the environment.

Suggestions for Further Reading

Karl and Katherine Amman, *Cheetah*. New York: Arco, 1985. This book provides firsthand observations about cheetahs in the wild and is accompanied by excellent photographs.

Gina Kopecky, "Life with Shallah," *Life,* October 1998. An account of raising cheetahs that illustrates the fine line between tameness and wildness in these animals.

Susan Lumpkin, *Big Cats*. New York: Facts On File, 1993. A well-organized and informative book for middle-school readers on the large cats, including the cheetah.

Ranger Rick, "New Chance for Cheetahs," September 1998. A close-up look at Laurie Marker and the work of the Cheetah Conservation Fund.

George B. Scahller, *Serengeti: A Kingdom of Predators*. New York: Knopf, 1972. A detailed description with plentiful photographs of the lives and interactions of cheetahs and their competition among predators.

Works Consulted

Books

Encyclopedia of Mammals. Vol. 4. New York: Marshall Cavendish, 1997. Probably the most thorough and most readable treatment of cheetahs in an encyclopedia format.

George Frame, *Swift and Enduring*. New York: E. P. Dutton, 1981. Firsthand observations and anecdotes about cheetahs are contrasted with stories of the slower but more enduring wildcats.

Bernhard Grzimek, *Grzimek's Encyclopedia of Mammals*. Vol. 3. New York: McGraw-Hill, 1990. This encyclopedia by a veteran German zoologist includes opinions that are somewhat different from standard fare on cheetahs.

Gunter Zeisler, *Safari*. New York: Facts On File, 1984. Another well-photographed, firsthand account about cheetahs in wilderness settings.

Periodicals

T. M. Caro, and M. Karen Laurenson, "Ecological Genetic Factors in Conservation: A Cautionary Tale," *Science,* January 28, 1994.

George W. and Lory Herbison Frame, "Cheetahs in a Race for Survival," *National Geographic,* May 1980.

Gina Kopecky, " Life with Shallah," *Life*, October 1998, p. 95.

Elizabeth, Pennisi, "Cheetah Countdown," *Science News,* September 23, 1993.

Kim Peterson, "Hope for a Speedy Recovery," *San Diego Union-Tribune*, October 20, 1999.

Susan Reid, "Cheetah's Champions," *People Weekly,* June 14, 1993.

Internet source

Cheetah Conservation Fund, *Newsletter #12,* July 1999. www.cheetah.org.

Index

Picture Credits

Cover photo: PhotoDisc
Corbis/© James L. Amos, 80
Corbis/© Tom Brakefield, 25, 34, 37, 42
Corbis/© W. Perry Conway, 8
Corbis/© Alissa Crandall, 24
Corbis/© Susan Middleton and David Liitschwager, 54
Corbis/© The Purcell Team, 50
Corbis/© Brian Vikander, 31
Courtesy Cheetah Conservation Fund, 62, 76, 79
© Tim Davis/Photo Researchers, Incorporated, 71
© Gregory G. Dimijian/Photo Researchers, Incorporated, 41
© John J. Dommers/Photo Researchers, Incorporated, 63
© John Giustina/FPG International, 52
© Hubertus Kanus/Photo Researchers, Incorporated, 60
© J. M. Labat/Photo Researchers, Incorporated, 78
© William and Marcia Levy/Photo Researchers, Incorporated,
   28
© Renee Lynn/Photo Researchers, Incorporated, 5
North Wind Picture Archives, 13
PhotoDisc, 10, 12, 18, 21, 27, 36, 38, 48, 58, 65, 67
© Mitch Reardon/Photo Researchers, Incorporated, 46
Martha Schierholz, 16
© Telegraph Colour Library/FPG International, 55

About the Author

Nathan Aaseng is the author of more than 150 books for young readers on a variety of subjects. His interest in the topic of cheetahs is inspired by one of his son's total fascination with wild animals. Aaseng from Eau Claire, Wisconsin, was the 1999 recipient of the Wisconsin Library Association's Notable Wisconsin Author Award.